This book is dedicated
to the memory
of
Christine Saxton
1945 - 1991

Contents

—— Acknowledgments ——

In the United States, and increasingly all over the world, people get information through the visual media. Because the visual media convey values, assumptions, and ideas, understanding how they work is important. This book introduces readers—who have most likely watched hours, months, even years of movies and television—to the vocabulary of film study and examples of interpretation. Knowing the appropriate terminology and basic methods of analysis will help viewers become media literate and develop a "critical eye."

To achieve these goals, this textbook presents descriptive examples accompanied by stills and concise film analyses. The beginning student can learn to recognize the way images and sound convey information and stories, to think critically, and to interpret the material. In short, the text should enable students to gain visual literacy and understand how movies produce meaning.

We would like to acknowledge colleagues and friends for the generous contribution of material: Jasmin Bodmer, Michael Collier, Nicole Hollander, Karen Holmes, Diane Kaye, Lynn Hershman Leeson, Helene and Matthias Neeracher, Carl Rosendahl, and Scott Simmon.

Chapter 1

Media Literacy

*A man is sharpening a straight razor on a strap. He steps out onto a
balcony, looks up at the sky, and sees a thin cloud moving toward the
moon. A young woman is seated in front of the man. His hand moves
slowly toward her face. The cloud glides across the face of the full moon.
The man grasps the razor, holds open the woman's eyelid, and slits open
her eye.*

The image on the cover of *The Critical Eye* captures the moment just
before the man slices the woman's eye in a startling close-up. The mysterious, melancholy face belongs to a little known French actor, Marie
Mareuil, in *Un Chien Andalou*, an avant-garde film made by Salvador Dali
and Luis Buñuel in 1928. Some seventy-five years later, the sequence is
as shocking as it was those many years ago. Dali and Buñuel, members
of the Surrealist art movement, meant to unnerve the viewer. They were
making explicit on screen their notion that the very function of film—of
all visual art—is to destroy old ways of seeing. Film and art must literally
open one's eyes. Their images surprise, shake up, and assault the viewer,
encouraging one to see differently, to perceive and think in new ways.
To see and hear from this changed perspective—to respond to image and
sound with analytical awareness—defines media literacy.

Literacy usually refers to reading: the term *literate* comes from the word
letter and has to do with words and language. To be functionally literate,

1

a reader must be able to grasp the meaning of each word, then of all the words combined, and, finally, to understand the meaning of a sentence and a paragraph. To be fully literate involves even more: the reader must be able to detect the underlying structure of a piece of writing, to recognize its persuasive elements, and to understand its implications. The ability to detect structure, recognize persuasion, and interpret implications is the basis of understanding all communication.

Although people grasp visual and aural information differently than written information, the terms *reading* and *literacy* may extend to film and media, as in "reading a film," "visual literacy," and "media literacy." The functionally media-literate viewer has the ability to understand sequences of moving images combined with sound, and to follow a story or understand information as conveyed through those visual and aural sequences. To be fully literate in media, a viewer also must be able to detect the structure of a work—whether it is a movie, TV commercial, news show, or sitcom—recognize the strategies of persuasion, and interpret underlying meaning. Full media literacy means the viewer has developed "a critical eye."

■ Worldwide Media and Communication

The media influence everyone, everywhere. Almost all of our lives, we have watched movies and television, mainly for entertainment and information. They are a source of pleasure, escape, even companionship — a constant part of the daily routine. But the media also have the power to influence and manipulate. The widespread power of the media has made it necessary to study, understand, and see how they work.

American culture has become influential worldwide. Hollywood movies have dominated foreign markets since World War I, and today the box office receipts of American films surpass the market share of local products. American television shows are distributed and popular around the world and have introduced new conduct and manners.

A 1999 report by Harvard Medical School researchers links the sudden infusion of Western cultural images and values, transmitted through television, to the way Fijian girls view themselves and their bodies. Fiji's single television channel broadcast such American programs as *Melrose Place*, *Beverly Hills 90210*, and *Xena, Warrior Princess*. In a survey taken 38 months after the introduction of television to the Pacific island, 74 percent of Fijian teenage girls reported feeling "too big or fat," 62 percent had dieted in the past month, and 15 percent had induced vomiting to control weight. As one schoolgirl in the study said, "We can see [teenagers] on TV. . . . They are the same ages, but they are working, they are slim and very tall, and they are cute, nice. . . .We want our bodies to become like that. . . so we try to lose a lot of weight." Three years of primarily American, British, and Australian television programming can be tied to the sharp rise in eating disorders and the penchant for Western beauty ideals encroaching upon the traditional Fijian preference for full-bodied shapes for both women and men.

Recently *Baywatch*, one of the most widely syndicated television programs in the world, has become a favorite with global audiences. Reaching 1 billion people a week in 140 countries and 33 languages, the episodes have been accused of contributing to problems for American women traveling abroad. The female lifeguards depicted on the show are positive role models: heroic, professional, and capable of making any rescue their male co-workers can make. But they also are represented as sexually available, and the camera often objectifies their scantily clad bodies with slow motion shots lingering on their breasts and legs. *Baywatch* sends the message that American women are promiscuous objects of desire. Such cultural stereotyping causes misconceptions that can foster harassment.

American television companies are pursuing markets in countries such as Portugal and Turkey, where distribution of TV programming is just emerging. In some established foreign markets, local productions are challenging the Hollywood product and causing licensing revenues to level off. In an attempt to regain market share, the major studios are designing shows specifically for individual national audiences and shooting them in those countries. These are immediate and widespread signs of American cultural influence. Subtler changes, such as the steady conversion of European television from a cultural to a merchandising entity, are also the result of American business practices governing media.

At another very important level, due to developments in telecommunications technology, information travels faster and farther than ever before. Satellite, wireless, fiber optics and cable networks speed information across national borders, creating a global network. The effect of this "migration of information" is incalculable.

In 1997 satellite technology permitted people throughout the world to watch the July 1 ceremony celebrating Hong Kong's return to Chinese sovereignty, an ironic reversal to the 1987 viewing of China's violent response to the Tiananmen Square demonstration. Viewers in many countries watched the fall of the Berlin Wall and the Persian Gulf War live on TV, which swayed popular opinion. Worldwide reaction to the breaking news events affected governmental responses and, therefore, government policy. According to some media analysts, the hastiness of German unification was largely the result of massive and emotional public response to images of the Berlin Wall being torn down (see fig. 1). When the former President of Poland, Lech Walesa, was asked what had caused the collapse of Communism in Eastern Europe, he pointed to a nearby TV set and replied, "It all came from there." The unprecedented number

Figure 1. Media analysts contend that the massive and emotional public response to images of the Berlin Wall being torn down in November of 1989 hastened German unification.

(Photograph by Diane Kaye, © 1989)

of people throughout the world who saw these and other events in their homes, who watch the Academy Awards or the Olympics, who tune in to MTV or surf the World Wide Web, demonstrates the vast horizons opened up by international telecommunications. Clearly a new era has arrived in which television and the Internet not only document and report events and trends, but also shape and accelerate them.

Through state-run media agencies, some countries control and limit what their citizens can see, thereby influencing and containing the population. But current technology can undermine strict government regulation. In Vietnam, which remains a one-party-rule nation with a communist ideology, a person can put a satellite dish on the roof and catch CNN, MTV, BBC and other Western sources of information. While bookstores and newspapers are governmentally controlled, video stores are not. Vietnamese viewers can rent everything from Hong Kong to Hollywood movies and consider the possibilities that exist in the outside world.

China is still largely a closed society, where the government restricts satellite reception and the media. Television broadcasts of overseas companies are limited to some tourist hotels and foreign residential compounds. But the Chinese have been quickly adopting the Internet, from universities to businesses to homes. The country's government estimates that Internet demand has tripled in less than 2 years, amounting to nearly 26 million users in 2001. Internet service providers in China are required to block Web sites considered subversive, and unlicensed Internet cafes are shut down. Soon software installed on a computer network outside the country may allow Chinese citizens to circumvent their government's central control, allowing print news, audio broadcasts, and e-mail newsletters to enter the nation without being censored. Such regimes are losing power over the media, primarily because the Internet is changing the face of information and entertainment, offering online users unparalleled opportunities for access and interactivity.

The role of the media in contemporary American society has expanded. Daily newspapers used to be the primary source of information to households, but today their total circulation has dropped. Now people depend almost exclusively on the visual media for both news and entertainment. Television has reached saturation in the domestic market: 99 percent of American homes have at least one color TV set, and the majority of households have two or more. According to the A.C. Nielsen Company, which monitors viewing habits, at least one TV was on in each of these homes for 7 hours and 37 minutes during the 1998-1999 season. This medium has become a considerable part of people's daily lives and affects the way those lives are led. As a result of the influence of television, movies, and the Internet, people all over the world are becoming part of a vast visual and aural culture as dependent upon looking at images combined with sound as on reading words.

■ Advertising, the Visual Media, and Persuasion

Advertisers know very well just how powerful an image can be. Ad agencies regularly spend millions of dollars on market research regarding audience preferences and responses to images, and have spent over $175 billion annually on ad campaigns catering to those preferences. Successful campaigns generate many more billions in return. Ads are designed to influence their audience. Not quite so obviously, movies and TV programs are also designed to influence their viewers. Like the consumers of food and drinks, audiences are increasingly seen as target groups, whose responses are tallied and quantified. If a market emerges among a statistical sample of "teens 14 to 17, living in urban areas, with a disposable income of $8000 a year," then films and TV programs geared specifically to that target group will very likely be produced.

The purpose of an ad is to sell a specific product. The purpose of a film is to sell itself. The purpose of a network television program is to sell both. TV is a vehicle for broadcasting paid advertisements in order to generate corporate profits, but it also sells in more subtle ways. Although the content of any single show may have little to do with a specific product, each program has the potential to model behavior by displaying attractive people in attractive settings. Viewers often imitate these fictional characters' attitudes and ideas, behavior and responses—desiring and acquiring the cars, cigarettes, clothes, and other products seen in the show.

Movies do not take commercial breaks, so they are less involved than TV shows with direct sales. However, for years the motion picture industry has used the more subtle advertising approach of inserting brand-name products into feature films. Product placement, as the practice is called, has become a big business. The brands of cars and merchandise used within the story are often given prominence in the framing of the shot. A product might be deliberately stressed through a single visual or verbal reference. For instance, the extra-terrestrial's fondness for Reese's Pieces in Steven Spielberg's *E.T.* (1982) boosted sales 62 percent. Other movies incorporate a brand-name product as part of the humor in a scene. Marty McFly (Michael J. Fox) orders a Pepsi Free in Robert Zemeckis's *Back to the Future* (1985), and the worm creatures smoke Marlboros at the coffee machine in Barry Levinson's *Men in Black* (1997). Sales of the $100 Ray-Ban wraparounds that Will Smith and Tommy Lee Jones wear in that blockbuster went up 300 percent after the movie's release.

Some films incorporate specific trademarked products into the narrative, aggressively promoting specific brands. Roger Spottiswoode's *Tomorrow Never Dies* (1997), the nineteenth James Bond film, pitches everything from cell phones to cosmetics. The producers made numerous product placements integral to the script in order for MGM/UA to obtain high-profile partners in a global marketing campaign. Bond (Pierce Brosnan) pursues villains while driving BMW's new 750iL sedan, escapes danger using his custom-built Ericsson cellular phone, and detonates bombs with his Omega Seamaster watch. The world's best-dressed secret agent runs from an explosion in a Brioni cashmere coat and orders cocktails made with Smirnoff vodka. His female co-star (Michelle Yeoh) uses L'Oréal's new 007 cosmetics line. The companies supplied the products and contributed to the $100 million marketing campaign because the film property was targeted to their own advertising goals. Perhaps the most overt promotion of a single corporation occurs in Robert Zemeckis's *Cast Away* (2000), which integrated the logo and services of Federal Express into almost every frame.

A new twist in the convergence of advertising and motion pictures has been taking place on the Internet. Although movie directors often make commercials, and movies have featured product placements for some time, well-known directors are now making digital short films that run exclusively on the Web site of the company whose product is being promoted. *The Hire*, a series of mini-dramas bankrolled by BMW (*bmwfilms. com*), is an example of the "advertainment" or "commission content" trend blending marketing and entertainment. Although all five shorts prominently feature a new BMW automobile driven by actor Clive Owen (*Croupier*), each six-minute spot has a different story line and serves as a signature piece for its director: John Frankenheimer (*Ronin*), Ang Lee (*Crouching Tiger, Hidden Dragon*), Wong Kar-wai (*In the Mood for Love*), Guy Ritchie (*Snatch*), and Alejandro Gonzalez Iñarritu (*Amores Perros*). The emerging online genre keeps the brand name before the viewer's eyes while delivering a creative, entertaining experience.

Feature films sell a lifestyle and, as much as any advertisement, depend on affecting an audience emotionally. In order to make money, movies must attract viewers to produce box-office revenue and promote merchandising tie-ins, to generate rentals and sales in video, laserdisc, and digital versatile disc (DVD) formats, and to secure television distribution deals. So, whereas ads work to produce meaning for the sole purpose of selling a sponsor's product, movies and television produce meaning for the purpose of involving viewers so as to keep them coming back.

The visual media resemble advertisements in that they use mainstream ideas about characteristics associated with people: femininity and masculinity, youth and age, race and ethnicity, beauty, success, and other attributes. When accepted ideas are embodied within characters in advertisements, television shows, and movies, the viewer quickly recognizes "types" and expects certain behavior from them. The point is powerfully illustrated by cigarette advertising. Marlboro ads associate cigarette smoking with rugged masculinity as represented by a cowboy. Virginia Slims presents the smoker as a young, active, independent woman. Benson & Hedges offers itself as the cigarette for a sophisticated and affluent group. Camel used a suave cartoon character to sell itself to the cool, hip consumer.

No one actually has to belong to any of the modeled groups. One only needs to want to belong and to want to be like the figures in the ads, to identify with them. The attraction and identification may be so great that a person will actually take up smoking no matter how deadly or illegal it may be. For years, cigarette manufacturer R.J. Reynolds denied that the Joe Camel character had been devised to capture underage smokers. However, in January 1997, internal company memos were made public that divulged the precise strategy for attracting young teenagers through the Joe Camel marketing plan: "fourteen-year olds are the future smokers." After the Joe Camel campaign was launched, the brand's share of the teenage market soared from almost nothing in 1988 to 33 percent in 1991, accounting for $476 million in sales. The R.J. Reynolds's teen-directed marketing was a big success but resulted in lawsuits that forced the tobacco company to halt Joe Camel ads nationwide.

The same persuasive techniques used to sell products have been applied to "sell" politicians. Former advertising writers, now calling themselves political consultants, carefully craft an image that markets candidates as though they were a brand of breakfast cereal. Former President George Bush was referred to as the "leading brand that had lost its popular appeal" when he went down to defeat in the 1992 presidential election which, incidentally, took place almost entirely on television. Media analysts contend that the 2000 presidential contest was more of an entertainment series than a serious discussion of issues. Candidates Al Gore and George W. Bush were positioned as celebrities and acted like performers, appearing on *Oprah, Live With Regis, The Tonight Show,* and *The Late Show With David Letterman.* They were expected to attract an audience by being entertaining, not by talking politics, like any guest with a new book or a new show to promote—only they happened to be marketing themselves as the next President of the United States.

To interpret an ad or assess a political candidate at a deeper level requires work, but the effort finally gives the viewer power to understand meaning and make an informed judgment. Although ads have a more direct purpose than either films or television shows, all of these forms treat characters, settings, and narrative in similar ways. Successful ads usually have good production values and are entertaining, and in some way appeal to the viewer's desires, fears, reason, or emotions. But each spectator's reception of these sights and sounds—the degree to which the viewer engages and interacts with media representations—varies depending on individual responses to the myths, values, and traditional assumptions of the culture and society.

■ The Narrative Film and Communication

What happens when we look at a film that tells a story? Does it show only what was in front of the camera? Do events happen in the film exactly as they do in real life? An examination of the beginning of Rob Reiner's *Stand By Me* (1986) reveals the complexity of its seemingly simple elements. The setting is realistic — the town looks like any small town — and the boys look like a group of ordinary kids (see fig. 2).

The opening establishes the scene with a wide view of fields and trees, a Toyota Land Cruiser parked on the side of the road in the distance. Suddenly "we" are closer to the car and then inside it, in the passenger seat, looking at the main character, Gordon (Richard Dreyfuss). In an instant we have somehow traveled at least a hundred yards, managed to reach the opposite side of the car and get inside. Equally remarkable,

Figure 2. Stand by Me (d. Rob Reiner, 1985). All elements make the shot realistic: ordinary-looking boys, simple clothes, no obvious make-up. The straight-on angle and medium shot reproduce a person's normal view. Linear perspective, marked by the diagonal of the railroad tracks, leads the viewer's eye back into the frame. The line of the tracks hints at the distance the boys have traveled and contrasts with the direction of the outstretched arm and the gazes.

Gordon's lips are not moving, yet we hear him speaking as he gazes out the front window of the car. The time-honored convention of the voice-over conveys his thoughts. While we hear him reminiscing about his past, another time-honored movie convention, the flashback, conveys his memories. Through an impossible leap in space and time, the scene shifts back about twenty-seven years to a little town in Oregon.

So far, the organization of the segment is fairly standard for narrative film, and we understand it perfectly well, since most of us have seen hundreds of flashback sequences and heard countless voice-overs. In fact, we are already "reading" the film. We grasp and accept this first part of the movie, even though it does not adhere strictly to reality, and we go on comfortably to the next part that takes place in Castle Rock, Oregon, in 1959. Here, too, at first the action seems to be recognizable and even more continuous, even more like "real life." Young Gordie picks up and pays for a magazine in a drugstore. But then we immediately find ourselves outside on the street, and Gordie is strolling out the door and coming toward us. How did he get from the cash register to the sidewalk so fast? And, for that matter, how did we get all the way down the street to look back at him? Clearly, even this most standard opening of a standard narrative film is not like real life.

Once viewers think about what they are seeing and hearing, they realize movie action and events really are not at all like their life experience. Movies only seem to be real because people have grown accustomed to seeing them through the camera eye and reading meaning into them within a story. Audiences have learned the conventions of narrative film. But most viewers understand only a little about what they see and hear. They do not detect structure, notice film editing, become aware of the sound design, or recognize that every image sets out to persuade. And if viewers never question what they see and hear and how it is presented, they are completely susceptible to the power of the media.

The opening scenes of *Stand By Me* show that even realistic sequences are not really "real." They are constructed from single shots that attempt to elicit very specific responses. The essential point is that all media are made up of bits of information bound together to produce a meaningful whole. All images and sounds are significant, and to understand that significance, viewers must investigate and process various kinds of information. If viewers do not understand the meaning of a single shot, they will not be able to put it together with others in a way that makes sense. Images must be read, and even a single shot—the simplest and most straightforward one—requires reading.

■ Levels of Meaning

One question remains: Why go to all the trouble to figure out underlying meanings when you can just sit back and enjoy the show? In-depth exploration can make watching films more interesting, more fun, and more useful. Almost all movies contain many more ideas and much more information than comes across on a superficial viewing. As with all the arts, the more you discover and understand about the aesthetic principles governing the work, the richer your experience of that work will be. And finally, a close examination leads to an understanding of how the media use values, social expectations, and widely shared beliefs and structures to affect viewers. If using the media is a source of power for politicians, advertisers, and film and television producers, then fully understanding the way those media work gives power back to the viewer.

Chapter 2

Elements of Meaning

✳[Films are one form of communication with a viewer, and one purpose of communication is to convey ideas. Most films tell a story, document an event, investigate a situation, persuade, convince, or explore an issue. To achieve this, the filmmaker must create meaning in a work and the viewer must extract it.]

How do filmmakers produce meaning? Filmmakers manipulate the materials and techniques available to them. They choose and structure such narrative elements as point of view, characterization, setting, and plot. They select the elements of cinematography including lenses, lighting, camera distance and angle, that is, the appropriate setup for a particular shot. They determine the *mise en scène* — arranging everything from color design to costumes, props to performers in front of the camera. They edit, assembling shots and sounds in a specific order. At all times, filmmakers must balance theme, narrative form, and elements of visual and aural representation.

Because filmmaking is a collaborative process, each project requires the contributions of many key people including a producer, screenwriter, director, cinematographer, production designer, sound designer, an editor, and very likely a special effects coordinator. Their active involvement varies during the course of making the movie, which is divided into three stages: preproduction, production, and postproduction.

In preproduction, the developmental stage before the shoot, the producer and writer figure prominently. The **producer** is the key player who controls the financing and making of the film, including putting together the "package" of script, director, and stars. The producer secures financial backing; develops or acquires "the property" or script; hires the director who then begins to oversee artistic issues; and approves the actors and crew. These negotiated contract agreements are above-the-line costs which sometimes include "pay or play" and profit-participation clauses. After these preliminary decisions have been made, the producer supervises the progress of the production, controls the schedule and expenditures, and handles other business details until the film has been completed and picked up for distribution. During the actual shoot, the **line producer** serves as the liaison between producer and director on everyday matters such as the production schedule and below-the-line costs, which range from equipment rental to hiring animal handlers. Although some producers have large staffs, many independents work alone out of an office in their home.

The **screenwriter** drafts a screenplay that serves as a blueprint for the film. Although the screenwriter's contribution of telling the story is of the utmost importance, few viewers can recall the name of the person who created the film's surprising plot twists, fascinating characters and memorable dialogue. Movie buffs can quote Marlon Brando's line from *On the Waterfront*—"I coulda been a contender"—but do not remember that Budd Schulberg wrote it. Screenwriter Joseph C. Stinson came up with "Go ahead, make my day" for *Sudden Impact*, not Clint Eastwood as Dirty Harry. And even though viewers know that cartoon character Jessica Rabbit could not possibly have created the classic line in *Who Framed Roger Rabbit*—"I'm not bad. I'm just drawn that way"—the names Jeffrey Price and Peter S. Seaman do not come to mind. These examples illustrate how even a small part of the screenwriter's work affects the success of a film and influences popular culture.

The writer's craft includes creating believable characters and dialogue, establishing the setting and tone, planning the structure and plot developments, and telling a story through images and sound. The scriptwriter may only have an idea to pitch to a producer or a detailed treatment that includes guidelines for the final script. Or the writer may provide a completed screenplay of approximately 120 pages for a 2-hour movie. Once the script sells, the screenwriter relinquishes all rights to the production company that purchased it. The producer can hire other writers to make revisions without consulting the person who first created the original screenplay. So some screenwriters write an entire script; others are hired just to rewrite or make major changes in the storyline, and still others only to polish dialogue or action.

The **director** takes charge of the production stage, the actual filming or principal photography, and makes decisions on the artistic rather than business end of the work. Four crucial areas must reflect the director's vision during the shoot: set design; costumes, make-up, and acting; cinematography and lighting; and special effects. Each of these divisions requires a crew of specialists and assistants. In most cases, the director also works with the producer and screenwriter during the preproduction stage, as well as with the original writer or subsequently hired script doctors to make necessary revisions during the filmmaking process. The director collaborates with the editor and sound designer, as well as the special effects team, during the postproduction phase.

Working closely with the **cinematographer** or **director of photography (D.P.)**, the director may determine the framing and setup of shots. But the D.P. must supervise the crew on highly technical matters involving film stock, lenses, gels or filters, lighting arrangements, and camera operation. The **production designer**, working under the director as well, oversees researchers, artists, and a crew of carpenters and decorators. Finally, the director deals with the actors, who are supported by costume designers and make-up artists.

The postproduction stage readies the film for distribution. During this final stage, the motion picture is edited, the soundtrack is mixed, and all special effects work completed. While the director supervises this stage as well, the producer often has the power to override the director's decisions. Once the film is finished or "in the can," a **distributor** markets the film and arranges for theatrical exhibition, television broadcast, and release on videotape, laserdisc, or DVD.

Some Hollywood directors have been deeply involved in more than one area of production: D.W. Griffith, Charlie Chaplin, Alfred Hitchcock, George Lucas, Francis Coppola, and Steven Spielberg have participated in writing, editing, and, above all, producing their own films to ensure creative control. Because independent filmmakers work with low budgets and often produce very personal works, they usually are active in all phases of the filmmaking process. Feature filmmakers John Sayles, Jim Jarmusch, and Kevin Smith, and documentary filmmakers Les Blank, Michael Moore, and Errol Morris direct, and often film and edit their own work, sometimes distributing it as well.

■ Film as Language

Early theorists of editing compared film to language, equating the shot to a word and the sequence to a sentence. They were not saying that shots were the same as words but rather that the shots interact with each other the way words do to produce meaning. Like words in sentences, shots gain meaning from their context. The Russian film director Sergei Eisenstein, writing in his seminal works *Film Sense* and *Film Form*, proposed a theory based on this analogy to language. He said that individual shots are only partial details of the whole and cannot stand alone. Shots work together to produce a cumulative meaning from a context, meaning not present in any single shot but emerging from all the shots put together. Understanding the material within each shot and within the context makes it possible to "read" the meaning of the entire film.

The idea that viewers understand film the way they understand language has gained some support over the years. Sophisticated theories on the relationship between language and film have been applied to account for the specifically visual quality of cinema: traditionally films show rather than tell information, and they do so in such a way that meaning is conveyed on several levels. One way to learn to "see" and "read" these various levels of meaning is to analyze the film text, breaking the work down into its component parts, looking carefully at those parts, and placing each into a larger context—shots within the sequence, the sequence within the whole film. Through examination, the interaction among all the elements becomes clear, the structure of the work takes shape, and meaning is revealed.

■ Underlying Meaning

Human experience is full of meaning. People spend much time making meaning through speaking, writing, and doing—or attempting to make sense of the meaning produced by others through listening, reading, and viewing. To make sense of written or visual material, people must interpret it, and to do so they must be able to use tools, in this case, methods of film criticism.

Meaning in a shot, sequence, or the entire film occurs at two levels: the literal level and the connotative level. **Literal meaning** may be defined as specific, exact information emerging from the images and dialogue. **Connotative meaning** is associative: feelings and ideas are linked with images and words, and information is hinted at or implied, or else arises from what the spectator brings to the material.

In both film and literature, the organization of a work and the repetition of elements within it develop themes, symbols, metaphors, motifs, and allusions. Meanings emerge from the film text, and, specifically, from the way image and sound are arranged to form a structure.

Casablanca offers an example of the way textual meaning develops. At the beginning, an orchestral piece is heard as background music. In an early scene, Ilsa (Ingrid Bergman) asks Sam (Dooley Wilson) to play the song "As Time Goes By" on the piano. Embarrassed, he refuses and then reluctantly begins to play. Rick (Humphrey Bogart), hearing the tune, comes over to the piano, and says, "I thought I told you never to play that . . ." Suddenly he catches sight of Ilsa. At this point, the viewer recognizes the tune as the background music but has no idea of the song's significance or why Rick does not want to hear it played. The first flashback reveals "As Time Goes By" was the song Sam played on the day of Rick and Ilsa's last meeting, before she stood him up. As the film progresses, the song takes on other levels of meaning: It represents Rick and Ilsa's last moment together, then their whole love affair including the romance of Paris and innocent times before the war, extends to represent Rick's love for Ilsa, and finally denotes memory, the recollection of all the things that one can never again have after time has passed (see fig. 3). Woody Allen recognized the implicit layering and texturing that makes *Casablanca* a cultural icon and paid homage to it in his 1972 comedy, *Play It Again, Sam* (see fig. 4).

Figure 3. Casablanca (d. Michael Curtiz, 1942). The last time Rick heard "As Time Goes By" was in the days before the fall of France. In this memory/ flashback every detail is in place.

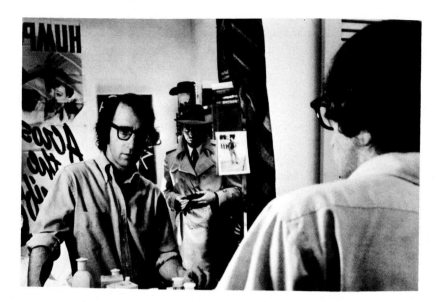

Figure 4. Play It Again, Sam (d. Woody Allen, 1972). "Bogart" reappears to counsel the protagonist in Woody Allen's homage to *Casablanca*.

■ Theme

The **theme** or multiple themes of a film are the main ideas that emerge as a function of the interplay among all the narrative, visual, and aural elements. Point of view, characterization, structure, symbolism, *mise en scène*, camerawork, editing, and sound—all aspects of a film—contribute to the theme.

Identifying a theme depends on understanding literal meanings and recognizing connotations. Viewers can watch most movies as entertainment and, with little effort, understand the plot. But recognizing connotations—the abstract dimensions associated with a person, action, image, or sound—requires a certain level of knowledge along with active participation by the spectator. Viewers can easily comprehend and recount the adventures of Dorothy Gale and her friends in *The Wizard of Oz* (1939). Yet most are unaware of the film's more abstract thematic, mythic, psychological, and ideological levels.

The interpretative aspect of film analysis is the most difficult one, because discovering the underlying meaning of a movie involves making connections between the world of the work and external ideas and experiences. Making these connections and extracting meaning from a film are not easy to do. Although many different critical approaches to film are available, this introductory text focuses on the basics of interpreting theme and understanding the elements that produce meaning.

■ Point of View

An essential element of narrative, point of view controls information by controlling the way information is conveyed and by affecting audience response. People commonly use physical and visual terms to express notions of point of view. "What position are you taking on that issue?" "He's taking a certain posture about all that." "I've got a whole new perspective on it." An author might take a stance on or have an attitude about the subject, story, or characters. Some expressions even parallel film terms. "What's your take on that?" "Here's my angle on that subject." "What's your frame of reference?" Point of view usually refers to opinions on a subject. In literature and film, however, **point of view** usually refers to the storyteller or the character who controls the story. The significant questions are: Who is telling the story? With whom do we empathize and identify?

When used in literary criticism, the term *point of view* is usually thought of as the eyes through which a character sees a story or an event. Literary critics, dedicated to definition and analysis of storytelling techniques, debate questions about point of view to better understand forms of literature, especially the novel. In novels the concern is with the narrator and ways of distinguishing between narrators who "see" (point of view) and those who "speak" (voice). The visual perspective can shape a story but so can the teller of the story.

Some basic issues arise about point of view in film as it relates to storytelling, suspense, and audience identification. Like writers, filmmakers must capture and hold the audience's attention, and to achieve that, they create narrative suspense. The filmmaker presents subject matter so that it provokes curiosity: "What will happen next?" **Suspense** is a state of uncertainty in which viewers experience apprehension or anxiety because they are encouraged to identify and sympathize with a character involved in a set of circumstances, to believe in the complications of the plot, and to agree with the outcome. Close-ups and subjective shots providing the character's point of view (discussed in Chapter 3) are major visual strategies that ally the viewer emotionally with the main character.

Written fiction has several possible narrators, some of which are also common in film. One way to recount a narrative is through the first-person narrator, the "I" who tells the story. Herman Melville's narrator begins his story in *Moby Dick* by introducing himself, "Call me Ishmael." Another form of narration uses the objective third person: she, he, or they. In this omniscient point of view, the author narrates and comments freely on the story: "Stately, plump Buck Mulligan came from the stairhead, bearing a bowl of lather on which a mirror and a razor lay crossed," says the outside observer narrating James Joyce's *Ulysses*.

In film the first-person narration usually involves a character who tells the story from his or her perspective, having lived through some or all of the experiences. The viewer must decide whether the narrator is reliable and worthy of identification in such films as *The Cabinet of Dr. Caligari*, *Mildred Pierce*, *Salt of the Earth*, *Rashomon*, *Little Big Man*, and *The Usual Suspects*. The narrator's credibility affects the way the viewer understands and responds to the content of these movies.

The device of the voice-over with dissolve described in Chapter 6 generally presents the first-person narrative. In the detective story *Murder, My Sweet* (made in 1944 from Raymond Chandler's novel *Farewell, My Lovely*), private investigator Philip Marlowe (Dick Powell) claims that he is being framed and begins to tell the police his side of the story. The present dissolves into the past, as Marlowe's voice continues over a flashback which shows the events in which he has become entangled. The device of the voice-over with dissolve "frames" the story.

Lady in the Lake (1946), adapted from another Raymond Chandler detective novel of the same name, experimented with the conventions of the first-person narrator. Director Robert Montgomery set out to reproduce Chandler's characteristic hard-boiled, first-person voice by allowing only subjective camera shots throughout the film. The camera "became" Marlowe and "saw" only what Marlowe could see—and so did the audience. Except for an occasional reflection in a mirror, the audience never sees an actor playing the hero. Therefore, identification becomes difficult because a camera is not very good at standard hard-boiled detective activities such as smoking, kissing, and fighting. A camera does a better job of showing action than participating in it. Yet it is interesting to study the use of the subjective camera on those rare occasions when it serves as the basis of an entire film.

Some theorists claim that all films really tell stories in the third person and, in fact, from a position outside any individual. The camera is a neutral, objective mechanism. In fact, in French the word for lens is *objectif*. Because the camera normally records action from an impartial, detached position, it can be considered an objective narrator. Even when the scene moves into a flashback that "belongs" to a character, once the events being recounted appear on the screen, the camera becomes the overriding observer and presents everything the viewer sees. Sometimes a character other than the narrator is associated with or assigned to a point of view shot that "belongs" to him or her. Almost all films include shots that represent the specific point of view of different characters.

■ Structure

The **structure** is the planned framework of a film. Whereas *mise en scène* organizes space within the shot, structure usually organizes time within a work. The structure emerges as the film unfolds—sometimes as a story or narrative, sometimes in essay form, sometimes in visual form. This arrangement of events or images significantly contributes to the theme.

After years of watching movies, television situation comedies, soap operas, and dramatic serials, most viewers are familiar with conventional narratives in fiction. Films resemble written narrative forms in certain ways: they all depend on characterization, setting, plot, and imagery.

The **plot,** a planned series of interrelated actions that develop and resolve a conflict, drives the film narrative. Every plot has opposing forces, a **protagonist** and an **antagonist**, struggling against each other in an arrangement of events that builds dramatic tension. Scenes may advance in chronological order, that is, sequentially according to the time of occurrence. The order may return to past events in a flashback or introduce future events in a flash forward, or events may occur simultaneously. In all cases, a cause-and-effect relationship must link one event to the next so that the story advances in a natural and logical manner. If any part of a tightly unified plot is changed or removed, the story will not work.

Most narrative films have a **three-act dramatic structure**. While establishing the tone, **Act One**, also called the set-up or exposition, introduces the characters and setting. A **catalyst** or inciting incident starts the action. In *The Wizard of Oz*, an unpleasant neighbor (Margaret Hamilton) obtains a sheriff's order to take Toto away from Dorothy (Judy Garland), because the dog had bitten her leg. She threatens to have the pet destroyed and to initiate a lawsuit that would give her possession of Aunt Em and Uncle Henry's farm. This upsetting incident induces Dorothy to daydream about a place "somewhere over the rainbow" where no trouble exists and then to run away with Toto. She rushes home when the traveling mind reader, Professor Marvel (Frank Morgan), says that her aunt has become very ill. Act One raises the film's central question: Will Dorothy get home to Aunt Em in time?

Act Two, known as the confrontation, deals with the major plot developments that introduce and intensify the conflict, building toward the climax. The first **plot point** begins Act Two, spinning the action into a new direction. As Dorothy rushes home, a tornado tosses objects into the air. One of them hits Dorothy on the head, knocking her unconscious in her bedroom. Then the tornado seemingly whisks Dorothy, Toto, and their home away from Kansas, depositing them in the land of the Munchkins right on top of the Wicked Witch of the East. The house kills the bad witch, freeing the little people from her spell. The Munchkins are so grateful that they give Dorothy the witch's magic ruby slippers. This angers the Wicked Witch of the West who immediately appears on the scene and demands the slippers. The first plot or turning point consists of this cluster of incidents: Dorothy dreams that she has been transported to the colorful land of Oz where she gains possession of the magical shoes coveted by the Wicked Witch of the West, who will do anything to get them.

The confrontation between Dorothy—the protagonist—and the Wicked Witch—the antagonist—complicates the central question that usually crops up again at the beginning of the second act: Will Dorothy get home? Because Dorothy is in unfamiliar and unsafe territory, the journey has become much more difficult. Often the first plot point raises the stakes and requires the protagonist to make an important decision. In this case, Dorothy decides to follow the Yellow Brick Road to the Emerald City, where the Wizard of Oz may tell her how to get back to Kansas. The Wicked Witch will try to prevent Dorothy from attaining her goal of returning home.

Act Two consists of a series of escalating crises or obstacles. Usually about halfway through the film, the protagonist is faced with a big challenge. At this **midpoint**, the protagonist renews his or her commitment of achieving the goal and reveals important character traits in doing so. This plot point truly challenges the protagonist, and the **story beats** — the major events in the story—begin to happen faster and make the narrative more exciting. Dorothy and her friends (Ray Bolger as the Scarecrow, Jack Haley as the Tin Woodman, and Bert Lahr as the Cowardly Lion) meet the great and powerful Oz. Before the Wizard will grant their requests, however, he insists they prove themselves worthy by bringing him the Wicked Witch's broomstick. Despite their fear of being killed by her, the foursome agree to the test.

The plot point that begins **Act Three**, also called the resolution, speeds up the action and makes the final act more intense than the other two. Sometimes a "ticking clock" is introduced to increase the tension. Then the narrative races towards the **climax**, the moment of greatest suspense, in which a single incident resolves the struggle between forces. The **falling action** and **resolution** tie up all the loose ends.

When the winged monkeys swoop down and carry Dorothy and Toto to the witch's castle, the third act begins. There the Wicked Witch realizes that her prisoner must be killed before the ruby slippers will come off her feet. She turns over an hourglass (the "ticking clock") to indicate how much longer Dorothy has to live. Toto's escape sets into motion a rescue attempt that leads to the final climactic confrontation. Disguised as guards, Dorothy's faithful friends enter the castle, release Dorothy, and come face-to-face with the green-skinned foe. The Witch lights the Scarecrow on fire, with the intent of killing the others next, and Dorothy grabs a bucket of water. She tosses the water at her friend but accidently douses the Wicked Witch. To everyone's surprise, the water makes the Wicked Witch melt away. With the antagonist destroyed and the broom in hand, the friends go back to Oz. The falling action deals with exposing the Wizard as a little man behind the curtain and learning how to get back to Kansas. In the resolution, Dorothy awakens from her dream surrounded by family and friends, and pronounces "There's no place like home." The central question raised in the first act has been answered.

When properly crafted, this type of dramatic structure draws the viewer into the story. It offers escapist entertainment, and the spectator responds to the material emotionally rather than in a thoughtful manner. The three-act dramatic structure encourages passive viewing and serves as the foundation of traditional Hollywood filmmaking.

Although narrative innovations have occurred throughout film history, a new generation of screenwriters and directors are telling cinematic stories in inventive ways. Time does not move in a straight line in Steven Soderbergh's *The Limey* (1999), which has a fractured narrative that effortlessly skips between the present and the past. Similar to Quentin Tarantino's *Pulp Fiction* (1994), Doug Liman's *Go* (1999) has multiple, intersecting story threads and toys with traditional notions of past, present, and future. German director Tom Tykwer's *Run Lola Run* (1999) replays the same narrative three times with slight variations that alter the outcome (see fig. 5). M. Night Shyamalan's *The Sixth Sense* and David Fincher's *Fight Club*, both released in 1999, give a clever twist to point-of-view issues. Not only does Christopher Nolan's *Memento* (2001) make the viewer question the reliability of the first-person narrator, who suffers from short-term memory loss, but the plot runs backwards. Logic is completely defied in Spike Jonze's *Being John Malkovich* (1999), which stars John Malkovich himself and takes place primarily in his brain. These narratives reflect the sensibility of those raised on technology that facilitates channel flipping with a television remote control, or cutting-and-pasting words and images with the click of a computer mouse, or sampling hip-hop—and all with the frenetic pace of videogaming.

Characterization shows each individual's motivation and development. A character may seem realistic with personality quirks, habits, and patterns of speech, but usually she or he also represents a philosophical position, psychological type, social class, and particular profession. In order to interpret the theme of a film, a viewer must consider the significance of the main characters. For the most part, the film protagonist and antagonist are defined by what they do. Action, not words or thoughts, usually reveals character. Who are the central characters? What do they represent? How do they and their situations change during the course of the narrative?

Three boxing movies illustrate how variations in characterization and structure can produce different themes in films of similar subject mat-

Figure 5. Run Lola Run (d. Tom Tykwer, 1998). Characterized by the frenetic pace and multiple narratives of a videogame, this German-language film reloads the same scenario three times with variations leading to different outcomes. Lola (Franka Potente) races against time to save her boyfriend (Moritz Bleibtreu) from the mob.

ter. In John Avildsen's *Rocky* (1976), the title character has a goal that motivates him to become a champ. As the linear story progresses, Rocky Balboa transforms himself from an underdog to an accomplished fighter through hard work and determination. Against all odds, the working-class hero wins fight after fight. Although Rocky does not win the championship fight, he wins a personal victory at the end and—wearing red, white, and blue—embodies the American Dream. The movie reinforces the notion that this country is a land of opportunity that offers name, fame, and fortune to hard-working individuals. John Huston's *Fat City* (1972) also has a linear structure that moves chronologically from start to finish. However, the theme is pessimistic and cynical because boxer Billy Tully wins his bout only because he fights an aging, unfit opponent. He loses his self-respect, abandons the ring entirely, and becomes a derelict. The negative turn to the story conveys a sense of life's futility and despair. As the narrator of Martin Scorsese's *Raging Bull* (1980), boxer Jake La Motta looks like an overweight has-been and seems simple-minded and slow. The frame structure flashes back to reveal La Motta's battles inside and outside of the ring. Shot in slow motion with a moving camera that places the spectator in the ring and, more specifically, in La Motta's mind, the fight scenes emphasize repeated, brutal blows to the prizefighter's head. This partially explains his tragic condition in the present, which was brought about by his self-destructive, violent lifestyle.

The **setting** is crucial to the film's meaning. It is defined as the place of the action and the time period: a historical moment, season, or time of day. **Imagery** refers to the way this physical space is depicted on screen (see fig. 6). Delmer Daves's *The 3:10 to Yuma* (1957) illustrates the importance of these two elements. A rancher, Dan Evans (Van Heflin), is about to lose his land because of a severe drought. He accepts the dangerous job of guarding an outlaw named Wade and putting him on the 3:10 train to the prison in Yuma only because he needs money to pay for water to irrigate his ranch. While Evans and Wade wait at the station, the outlaw tempts the farmer with promises of thousands of dollars if Evans allows him to escape. Evans's struggle with temptation becomes a nearly biblical contest between "Satan" and "a good man" over possession of the man's

Figure 6. The Grapes of Wrath (d. John Ford, 1940). The classic narrative film, adapted from John Steinbeck's famous novel, preserves the era of the Depression as setting. Tom Joad (Henry Fonda) is both reflected in the mirror and separated from his family by its frame, foreshadowing his forced parting. The imagery literally reflects the theme.

soul. By including the drought as an element in the narrative, a second conflict is introduced, the contest between life and death: neither humans nor the land can survive without water. The desolate setting and stark imagery show the bleakness of life in the West, which is portrayed as a wasteland. The interaction of plot, characterization, setting, imagery, and sound—all the narrative and visual elements—produces meaning in the film.

Experience with stories leads to expectations of what a story should be. These expectations develop, in part, because certain kinds of stories appear again and again. Most narrative films fall into a **genre**, a set of stories containing predictable elements or conventions. Genre stories are so familiar that viewers know what to expect from a film advertised as a Western, detective movie, gangster film, science fiction film, horror film, or melodrama (see fig. 7). The viewers of a Western can expect to see settlers, horses, rifles, and wide-open spaces set in a particular time of American history. They can expect a conflict between cowboys and Indians, or sheepherders and cattlemen, or ranchers and land developers.

*Figure 7. **Bonnie and Clyde*** (d. Arthur Penn, 1967). Easily recognizable as a gangster film but, because of its setting in the rural west during the Depression, the movie also recalls the Western and the 1930s social commentary genres.

Seminal films within the Western genre include *Stagecoach, High Noon, Shane, The Searchers, Little Big Man* (see Chapter 7), and *Unforgiven*. Hollywood has relied on film genres because audiences enjoy them and pay to see them, and because tried-and-true formulas are less risky to finance and market than something new and different.

A number of films do not fit into genre categories, mainly because they are not based on formula. In these films, themes are shaped out of a delicate balance among the component parts. Although these works raise social, political, and psychological questions, they almost always relate stories that illustrate authentic human experience. Their themes draw on ideas and images that are both individual and universal, and their stories are developed in such a unique, complex manner that they defy the conventions and limitations of a three-act dramatic structure. Many classic films belong to this group, among them *Citizen Kane, The Rules of the Game, Grand Illusion, Children of Paradise*, and *Rashomon*.

▪ Symbol

A **symbol** is any image, object, character, setting, or sound charged with meaning beyond its usual definition. It is something concrete that stands for an abstract idea (see fig. 8). Almost all cultures consider water to be a symbol representing fertility and growth. In *The 3:10 to Yuma*, the natural phenomenon of drought, which has triggered the plot, takes on the classical symbolism of barrenness, a punishment for the townspeople's indifference to the spread of evil. As Evans struggles with his conscience, and ultimately conquers his temptation to behave dishonestly, clouds gather and lightning strikes. Finally when he arrests the evil by placing the criminal on the train, rain begins to fall, symbolizing purification, redemption, and the return of life-giving forces to the land.

The image of water, as well as that of fire, the circle, the sun, and certain colors are often recognized as **universal symbols**. These symbols evoke associations that have been understood across geographical boundaries and throughout history. Psychologist Carl Jung wrote that people share a collective unconscious in which universal symbols and archetypes emerge in myths, religions, dreams, fantasies, and art, and tap profound human emotion on a primal level. Expanding upon Jung's theories, scholar Joseph Campbell developed a concept of comparative mythology. His seminal work, *The Hero With a Thousand Faces*, traces the patterns underlying all the great myths such as the hero's quest and the hero's journey from innocence to enlightenment. The concepts strongly influenced George Lucas, who used them as the foundation of the *Star Wars* trilogy.

Figure 8. The Seventh Seal (d. Ingmar Bergman, 1956). The knight (Max von Sydow) plays chess with Death (Bengt Ekerot), his life at stake. The chess game is a symbol of the game of life. He might "put Death in check" this time, but ultimately he must lose the game. As the film progresses, Death takes the characters one by one, much as a chess player captures and removes his opponent's pieces.

Not all symbols are universal. Some emerge as symbols specific to a culture and may be called **cultural symbols**. They are those objects, ideas, and notions based on the general knowledge people gain about living and behaving in a particular society. Cultural symbols evolve from communal values, collective assumptions, and shared expectations. The standard film genres—Westerns, horror films, science fiction films, among others— express these conceptions within the conventions of their respective forms.

All cultures are associated with objects that take on specific symbolic meanings, from the national flag that represents the country to emblems with narrower signification. The Eiffel Tower represents Paris, while the Empire State Building represents New York City and the Golden Gate Bridge represents San Francisco. The figure of "Uncle Sam" stands for the United States, while "John Bull" stands for England. These are the simplest of cultural symbols. Most are more complex.

Because they emerge out of a specific social context, cultural symbols do not mean the same thing to all people. For example, in the United States the image of an elephant may stand for the Republican party, but to the Hindus the elephant is a religious symbol. Indeed, the symbols of one culture may not even be understood by people in another: the image of "fire in a lake" means revolution and change according to Chinese philosophy, but few Westerners know that. The meaning of the symbol depends on the definition the culture gives to it. Needless to say, a lack of knowledge prevents recognition of symbols in other cultures. On the other hand, American cultural symbols are often so familiar that their meanings seem natural, while their deeper implications often remain invisible.

When symbols materialize through repeated appearances or references in a specific text, they are called **textual symbols**. Objects and sounds may symbolize a character within the story: a battered hat or a distinct whistled melody may refer to a character. A close-up, a musical theme, lighting, framing, dialogue, or editing may direct the audience's attention to the symbol. Textual symbols develop out of the images and soundtrack of the film "text." Viewers perceive or read these single instances, note them and then when they recur, put them together to make sense of them (see fig. 9). In that respect, a symbol may be woven into a pattern or motif. For example, in *Citizen Kane*, jigsaw puzzles are referred to or seen in isolated instances throughout the film, but the concluding sequence presents the full symbolic meaning visually and in the dialogue. As reporters gather in one of Xanadu's great halls and look over the collection of Charles Foster Kane's belongings, Thompson idly handles some cardboard puzzle pieces in a box, admitting he has not solved the meaning of Kane's dying word "Rosebud." Asked what he has been doing all this time, he replies that he has been "playing with a jigsaw puzzle." A crane shot moves into an overview of the hall crowded with crates, statues, paintings, all the objects Kane had collected during his lifetime, which now look like the jumble of an unsorted puzzle. The point is made: the puzzle symbolizes Charles Foster Kane's life.

■ Motif

A **motif** is developed and elaborated by repetition and woven throughout a work. An object, visual or graphic pattern, narrative situation, phrase of dialogue or music, or sound effect may become a motif. For example, Bernardo Bertolucci's *The Last Emperor* (1987) has a bicycle motif. In China before the First World War, the bicycle was considered a toy of the upper classes. In the film, the Emperor Pu-Yi's English tutor rides a bicycle in the palace. Later the young Pu-Yi insists upon acquiring a bicycle,

Figure 9. Psycho (d. Alfred Hitchcock, 1960). The mirror, a textual symbol, divides and fragments the frame and reflects Marion Crane's (Janet Leigh) "darker" side. The framing objectifies her inner conflict over the theft of the money that she now holds in her hand.

learns to ride, and attempts to use it to escape the prison that the palace has become for him. At the conclusion of the film, after Pu-Yi has been integrated into Communist society, hundreds of bicycles ridden by the city dwellers are seen. The bicycle, once a symbol of the West, the upper classes, and progress, has become a mode of transportation for the masses —assimilated, like Pu-Yi himself, into modern Communist China.

Each time the object or element recurs in the film, the motif develops and lends meaning to and gains meaning from the whole work. In *Winchester '73*, the opening shot is a close-up of a perfect specimen of the famous rifle of the title, which is to be the prize in a shooting competition. Lynn McAdam (James Stewart) wins the gun, but his rival "Dutch Henry" Brown steals it from him. Subsequently the Winchester is stolen by an Indian chief, an Army private, and a hoodlum until its rightful owner finally regains it. The rifle takes on increasing significance as an instrument that provokes unchecked desire and breeds violence and death.

In *The Sixth Sense*, the color red is associated with the supernatural world. Any object that has a connection to the other side is crimson: the doorknob to the basement, the birthday balloon that leads Haley Joel Osment's character up the winding staircase to the attic (where ghosts slash his red sweater), his tent, the dress of the murderous mother at the funeral, the box holding the dead girl's videotape. The boy often "sees dead people" covered in blood. Providing visual clues, the color motif links bloodletting and violence to ghosts before an incident occurs. Red subtly foreshadows events in this well-crafted thriller.

■ Metaphor

Filmmakers use metaphors to point out similarities in seemingly dissimilar things. In language and literature, a **metaphor** is a figure of speech stating that one thing is another thing which, in fact, it is not. At the end of Spike Lee's *Malcolm X* (1992), African-American fourth graders take turns standing up in their Harlem classroom, emphatically announcing, "I'm Malcolm X." A sequence follows in which four South African students say the same thing. None of them, of course, is actually Malcolm X. Rather the students are comparing the qualities of the slain black leader to themselves: through education, they have learned about their African roots and culture, and thereby have gained a sense of self-respect, self-worth, and personal empowerment.

Some filmmakers use film techniques to express a metaphor in visual language. Sergei Eisenstein depicts a factory spy as a crafty animal in *Strike!* (1924) by first showing his face and then slowly dissolving to the head of a fox; this use of the dissolve is equivalent to saying "The man is a fox." At the end of this film, Eisenstein intercut the massacre of the striking factory workers with the graphic slaughter of an ox, creating a metaphor through editing that comments on the butchery of so many innocent people. The great Soviet director used poetic film language in all of his movies by arranging visual images in such a way as to suggest abstract metaphorical ideas in both simple and complex forms.

■ Allusion

An **allusion** is a direct or indirect reference to a person, place, or event external to the work in which it appears. It may be a reference to classic literature, another film, or to a topical event. Allusions are common in films, and are regularly used to extend the level of meaning beyond the visual presentation of the story. They may be brief asides, tributes to earlier films and filmmakers, humorous or cultural references. Woody Allen's *Bananas* and Brian De Palma's *The Untouchables* allude to Eisenstein's Odessa Steps sequence in *The Battleship Potemkin* (1925). The final shots of Steven Spielberg's *Raiders of the Lost Ark* (1981) recall the equivalent shots of *Citizen Kane*: as though searching for the key piece of a jigsaw puzzle, the camera cranes over thousands of crates in a United

States government warehouse where the Ark of the Covenant has been hidden and then lost. The sequence alludes to the closing shots inside Kane's Xanadu, while making a pointed comment about the bureaucracy of the American government.

All the elements defined in this chapter—theme, point of view, structure, symbol, motif, metaphor, allusion—contribute to the meaning of a film. The ability to identify these elements and extract meaning from them requires training, tools and methods for critical analysis, and the active participation of the viewer.

Chapter 3

The Camera Eye

A filmmaker's camera can be compared to a writer's pen or a painter's brush: the tool with which the artist expresses thoughts and feelings. French film critic and theorist Alexandre Astruc proposed the concept of the *caméra-stylo* in an influential essay published in *Ecran Français* in 1948. Through visual imagery, a filmmaker can establish a personal style that serves as "a means of expression as supple and subtle as that of written language."

■ The Camera

It really does not matter if a camera is analog or digital, 35mm or 16mm, video or high-definition 24P digital video. At the most basic level, a camera is a recording device. The motion picture **camera** mechanically records an image onto a plastic strip coated with a light-sensitive material called **emulsion**. But movie cameras do not reproduce movement at all. Instead they photograph still images that produce the illusion of movement when shown in rapid succession: 18 frames per second for silent film and 24 frames per second for sound film. The illusion is based on two characteristics of visual perception, one called the **phi phenomenon** and the other called **persistence of vision**. The brain retains an image cast on the retina of the eye for a split second after the image dis-

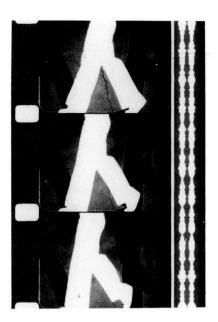

Figure 10. Saving the Proof (d. Karen Holmes, 1985). Two characteristics of visual perception, the phi phenomenon and persistence of vision, allow the viewer to see a series of static images as continuous movement because the brain retains an image cast on the retina for a split second after the image disappears.

appears from sight and allows the viewer to see a series of static images as a single, continuous movement. These two principles are actually responsible for the perception of movement in movies (see fig. 10).

Instead of capturing images in the photochemical grains of film emulsion, **digital video** or **DV** cameras register images as binary information — data that can then be computer-manipulated with ease. Standard digital video produces 30 interlaced images per second. When converted to film, 30 frames of information must be placed into 24 frames of film stock. In the process, some image data is lost, resulting in stuttering and unnatural blurs of color called artifacts. The 24P format solves this problem, because this digital video camera records 24 progressive frames per second similar to the 24-frame rate offered on 35mm film.

The viewer can see only what the director has chosen to record through the camera lens and save when editing. That statement may seem self-evident but when watching a movie. in this "age of mechanical reproduction," the audience may think that objective reality is being filmed without human intervention. It is easy to forget that the filmmaker's choices determine what finally appears on the screen. The fact is that the viewer "goes" only where the camera goes and "sees" only what and how the camera sees.

What the spectator sees is determined by several factors. Before a director and cinematographer even consider turning on a camera, they must decide what **gauge** or **format** to use. Although most theatrical releases are shot in the 35mm film gauge or format, sometimes a director chooses to shoot in 16mm, Super 16mm, or on video and then blow up the print or transfer the tape to 35mm for distribution. Because shooting in a lower-gauge or video format is less expensive, many independent filmmakers select one of these options to save money. Robert Rodriquez sold his $7,000 *El Mariachi* (1993) to Columbia Pictures on video, and then the studio spent a million dollars readying the low-budget production for theatrical release. A number of recent commercial features were shot by major film-makers on digital video: *The Blair Witch Project, Bamboozled, The Celebration, Dancer in the Dark, Time Code, Final Fantasy,* and *Episode II* of the *Star Wars* saga.

Some directors have aesthetic reasons for choosing a format other than 35mm. Mike Figgis fought to have *Leaving Las Vegas* (1995) produced in Super 16mm. He argued that the smaller, less obtrusive camera would capture more subtle expressions in the actors' faces and the 35mm blow up would make the print grainier, thereby enhancing the gritty realism of the film. Spike Lee made the same choice for the same reasons for *Get on the Bus* (1996), his fictional account of a group traveling to that year's Million Man March in Washington, D.C. For many filmmakers, digital video offers freedom and flexibility. The burden of large crews, elaborate lighting equipment and tedious setups is eliminated, allowing filmmak-ers to "run and gun" and revise works in progress on everyday computers. The director and cinematographer make format decisions based on what best supports the project's aesthetics and works for their budget.

If shooting on film, the type of **film stock** selected will affect the look of the subject. Fast film stock, for instance, is highly sensitive to light. Its emulsion can record images under low-light conditions, which allows the cinematographer both flexibility and the ability to achieve increased depth of field. Fast film stock can make deep-focus photography possible, but it also may produce grainy, high contrast images. Although well suited for the harsh world of *film noir* and for documentaries, fast film stock may be an inappropriate choice for filming upbeat musicals or comedies. Slow film stock, which requires more light and captures a softer image, sets the correct tone for these genres. John Bailey, who shot *Mishima* and many other features on 35mm and *The Anniversary Party* on DV, feels that cel-luloid has more latitude, subtlety in contrast and chroma range, and sharpness than tape. Another important consideration is whether to shoot in black and white, color, or a combination of both.

Once the director decides on a film or video format and the appropri-ate film stock or tape, production can begin. The **setup** of a shot, a process involving several steps, basically determines what the viewer sees. Usu-ally the director and cinematographer start by deciding where to place the camera—how close, how far, how high, how low. Then they decide how to shoot—when to move or not to move the camera, and especially, what kind of movement to use (see fig. 11). The possibilities are extensive, and the choices turn out to be very significant.

In the early days of cinema, action was shot from a fixed distance relative to the subject. Because directors could not easily move bulky 35mm cameras, they rarely did so unless a better view of the action and the background was needed. But very quickly, pioneering directors like Thomas Ince and D.W. Griffith realized that the angle on and the distance from the subject changed how the scene and the actors looked. These choices affected both the viewers' understanding of the story and their response to it. Directors soon began to plan camera placement with great care. To achieve meaningful results, they filmed from many angles and distances. They juxtaposed differing shots that gave the viewer the illusion of moving, freely and invisibly, among the characters, on the set, often at the very center of the action. Varying angle and distance marked an enormous leap in film language that continues to be important to the present day.

Figure 11. Alfred Hitchcock directs a take during the making of *Rear Window*. The setup established the camera angle and distance, and the lights and microphone placement. The set decor lends realism to the *mise en scène*, the arrangement of all the elements in front of the camera.

■ The Shot and the Frame

The **shot** is the primary unit of filmmaking and is usually defined as a single, uncut length of film that records an action without interruption; the **pixel** is the basic unit of digital video which can be manipulated with computer technology. The **frame** refers both to the edges of the image, which act like a picture frame, and to a single image. Carrying out the director's ideas, the cinematographer composes the image within the limits of the frame. She or he chooses the subject and frames it through the choice of lens, distance, angle, and lighting. These decisions emphasize details of action, character, and mood. In video the image tends to be centered rather than framed or captured casually in the run-and-gun approach.

■ The Lens

Controlling the size, scope, and range of focus, the choice of lens will affect the look and the meaning of the filmed material. The three basic lenses are the normal, wide angle, and telephoto. A **normal lens** uses a mid-range focal length and produces minimal distortion, approximating the scope and size of normal vision. Most often used for medium shots, its range of focus and depth of field are not as great as that of the wide-angle lens.

The **wide-angle lens** requires a short focal length and produces an image of great scope, or breadth, covering more of the subject. Figures near the camera will be quite large, while things will look smaller very abruptly when they are farther away from the camera. **Depth of field** is a measure of the extent of acceptably sharp focus. In motion pictures, depth of field can be increased by shooting with a wide-angle lens, and shutting down the lens aperture to reduce the amount of light hitting fast film stock that is extremely light sensitive. This combination makes the **deep-focus shot** possible, allowing action in all three planes—the foreground, middleground, and background—to be in focus at the same time (see fig. 12). Tape generally captures a flatter image.

In *Hope and Glory* (1987), director John Boorman uses a deep-focus shot to show a boy returning to school, walking dejectedly along the dark stone wall of the school yard. Framed by the gate, he enters the schoolyard, looks around, and sees his schoolmates going wild—cheering, leaping and throwing their books in the air. Behind them is a haze of smoke and dust, the school having been hit by German bombs. The deep-focus shot allows three significant and related pieces of information to be presented at once: the boy's reaction in the foreground, the response of the other students in the middleground, and the bombed-out buildings in the background.

Figure 12. The Magnificent Ambersons (d. Orson Welles, 1942). A wide-angle lens photographs the mansion's ballroom in a deep-focus shot. All the planes are in focus from the Christmas tree at foreground left, through the musicians in shadow and the rolled-up rug in the mid-foreground, to the older couple dancing in the middleground, to the young couple seated on the stairs in the background. Even the plants and wall lighting fixtures in the extreme background are in sharp focus. The low-key lighting draws the viewer's eye first to the center of the frame and then to the vanishing point.

The **telephoto lens** has a long focal length and is like a telescope magnifying the subject. Because the telephoto lens only produces sharp focus in one distance plane, the subject is isolated from its surroundings, which remain out of focus. It produces minimum depth of field which flattens the image and seems to trap a moving subject in the middleground. Toward the end of *The Graduate* (1967), Ben (Dustin Hoffman) races to get to the church before his true love Elaine (Katharine Ross) marries someone else. In a telephoto shot, Ben appears to be running frantically in place, showing great effort and little progress.

Filters or **gels**, which distort the quality of light entering the camera lens, influence the look and feel of a shot. They can trap and refract light to make an image sparkle, suppress or heighten certain colors, make daytime appear as night, and give actors and actresses a more glamorous look. Digital effects can render similar results in postproduction.

Focus is the degree of sharpness of the image. **Rack focus** or **pulled focus** is the term for changing the focus without stopping the camera. Images in one plane are sharp initially but gradually blur as focus is "pulled" to bring detail in another plane into focus. This technique is used when the director wants to shift attention from a character or object in one distance plane to another during the same shot. John Sayles used rack focusing in *City of Hope* (1992) for a sequence in which two policemen talk together in a squad car. Instead of relying on the shot/reverse shot sequence of cutting between the characters during a conversation, he relied on rack focusing to alternate the sharp focus as each character speaks.

In a **zoom shot**, a lens of variable focal length allows the cinematographer to shift between wide-angle and telephoto shots in one continuous movement. The resulting effect gives the viewer the impression of moving through space toward or away from a character or object. The zoom can either keep the entire framed image in focus or isolate a figure against out-of-focus surroundings. A fast zoom can be used to create a nearly physical effect in the viewer, since it makes space seem to rush toward or away from the camera. In *Vertigo* (1958), Hitchcock wanted to convey the main character's fear of heights. As Scottie Ferguson (James Stewart) looks down, the camera zooms in on the ground below while dollying out, creating the sensation that he—and the viewer—are plunging downward.

Figure 13. 2001: A Space Odyssey (d. Stanley Kubrick, 1968). In the close-up of David Bowman's (Keir Dullea) face, the helmet and the patterns of shadow reflected on it give the shot a rich texture, while limiting the area of the frame and emphasizing his facial expression. The close-up encourages identification with the character.

■ Distance

Depending on what information or emotion is to be conveyed, the film-maker will decide on the **camera distance**: a close-up, a medium shot, or a long shot. The distances of these shots are always relative to one another but measured according to human scale, that is, by how much of the human figure is registered within the frame. Filmmakers typically define degrees of distance.

In a **close-up**, the camera records an area in which a person's head or an object fills the screen with little or no background visible. In fiction films, the close-up is most often used to show a character's feelings, responses, and emotions or to show details or objects of special significance —a gun or cup of poisoned coffee. In documentaries, the close-up is used to "get close" to people interviewed and also to show details of objects or processes important to the subject matter being filmed. In both cases, the close-up contributes to the meaning of an image by conveying a feeling of intimacy and intensity (see fig. 13).

In a **medium shot** the camera records an area equal to the height of a seated figure or a figure from the waist up. This shot is commonly used for scenes in which the dialogue is important and a limited context is no obstacle (see fig. 14). In the classical period of the 1930s and 1940s, American directors frequently used a shot that they called a medium shot but

Figure 14.
Dark Victory
(d. Edmund Goulding, 1939). Bette Davis and Geraldine Fitzgerald are shown in a medium shot, the height of a seated figure. Filmed in an unobtrusive style, the two-shot is realistic: the medium distance and a normal lens approximate normal vision.

Figure 15. The Rocky Horror Picture Show (d. Jim Sharman, 1975). In a spoof on monster movies, Janet (Susan Sarandon) and Brad (Barry Bostwick) take shelter among the weird inhabitants of Frank N. Furter's house. The long shot allows the actors to use the whole body for comic expression.

which is actually slightly fuller as it includes the figure from below the knees.

The camera records an area that is the height of a standing figure in a **long shot**, usually including extensive background to emphasize the relation between the figure and its surroundings. The **full shot** is a more confined type of long shot, one in which a figure fills the screen from the top to the bottom of the frame. At that distance, the actors can make their physical stance and gestures noticeable and, at the same time, the camera is still close enough to display their facial expressions (see fig. 15).

These are the most common definitions of distance. In practice distinctions are made depending on the cinematographer's preferences and style. The list of definitions can extend to include the **medium close shot**, which is between a close-up and a medium shot, the **extreme long shot**, which produces a tiny figure in a great expanse of background, and the **extreme close-up**, which shows an enlarged detail of a face or an object.

■ Angle

Along with selecting the appropriate distance, the filmmaker must decide on angle. The **angle** is the position of the camera in relation to the subject. The camera and, therefore, the shot may be at eye level, low angle, or high angle.

The **straight-on, eye-level** shot seems to show no visible angle. Because the shot is used so often, it seems neutral or unbiased, reproducing the scope that corresponds most closely to the way that the viewer normally sees.

In the **low-angle shot**, the camera is placed lower than the subject, producing a towering form. This shot is used expressively to suggest the subject's dominance, power, or authority and, depending on the goal of the director, may create a heroic, menacing, oppressive, or mythic effect (see fig. 16). At one point in Orson Welles's *Citizen Kane* (1941), the young Charles Foster Kane opens a Christmas gift from his guardian, Mr. Thatcher. Charles looks up. The camera tilts up, representing the view of a little boy overpowered by his guardian, and holds in a low angle on Thatcher, who is looking down at the child.

Figure 16. *Citizen Kane* (d. Orson Welles, 1941). In this oblique angle or tilted shot, taken from a low angle, Charles Foster Kane (Orson Welles) is dwarfed by his campaign poster, just as the man is by the image he has created of himself.

An expressive use of the low-angle shot occurs in the scene of an attempted lynching in John Ford's *Young Mr. Lincoln* (1939). Lincoln is standing on the jailhouse steps, holding back a mob determined to hang the suspect. Ford shoots Lincoln from a low angle, suggesting the point of view of the mob that is looking up at the tall man. The low angle makes Lincoln look powerful and much larger than life; his successful check on the lynch mob reinforces his mythic stature.

John Frankenheimer's 1962 film, *The Manchurian Candidate*, contains several examples of the way extreme low angles produce tension and menace. Raymond Shaw (Laurence Harvey) is seen in low angle just before he carries out, under hypnosis, the command to kill his father-in-law. His oppressive, domineering mother, Mrs. Iselin (Angela Lansbury), is shown in several extreme low-angle shots that suggest her power over her son.

Another example of the use of the low-angle shot to produce a feeling of menace appears in Brian De Palma's *The Untouchables* (1987). Al Capone (Robert De Niro), framed in a low angle, moves slowly around a table at which his gang is seated. He pretends to be talking to them about baseball, but he is really talking about loyalty and teamwork. He ends his comments by using the bat that he is carrying to crush the skull of one of the henchmen whom he considers a traitor, as he finally carries out the menace that the low camera angle has been threatening.

In the **high-angle shot**, the camera is placed higher than the subject, often suggesting helplessness and vulnerability (see fig. 17). In *Psycho* (1960), Alfred Hitchcock used a high-angle shot for the murder of detective Arbogast (Martin Balsam). In the scene, the detective searching for the missing woman mounts the stairs of the old house behind the Bates Motel. The camera cuts from a straight-on shot of him climbing the stairs to a high-angle shot looking down at him. A figure swoops at him and stabs him. A cut to a high-angle shot shows him as he falls backward down the stairs, bleeding. The high angle makes the unsuspecting Arbogast look vulnerable to attack, heightening the menace and suspense set up by the brutal murder in the shower.

In the **extreme high-angle shot** or **bird's-eye shot**, the camera is placed directly overhead, perched "like a bird," looking straight down at the scene. The shot distorts the image slightly because the angle foreshortens perspective and, since people rarely see from that angle, it is not often used except expressively. Again *Psycho* offers two incisive examples. The first signals the murder of Arbogast. As the detective reaches the top of the stairs, a cut moves to a shot from a "bird's-eye" position. A figure moves at Arbogast from screen right, knife in hand, and attacks. The second use of the bird's-eye shot repeats the sequence of the first use but with differences. The shot comes several scenes after the detective's murder. This time Norman Bates (Anthony Perkins) goes up to his mother's room.

Figure 17. The Battleship Potemkin (d. Sergei Eisenstein, 1925). A group of women plead with Cossack soldiers to stop the massacre on the Odessa Steps. The high-angle shot looks down on them, emphasizing their vulnerable position.

The camera holds while Norman climbs the stairs. After he enters her room and is no longer in the shot, the camera continues to hold on the empty staircase, then begins slowly moving upward. The camera cranes up, past the open bedroom door, then rotates 180 degrees to hold, high above the landing, as Norman comes out of his mother's room, carrying her. Hitchcock's stated reason for using the bird's-eye view in the first case was to prevent the audience from seeing the murderer before the director was ready to reveal "whodunit." By using the bird's-eye shot in the second case, the director prevents the audience from seeing what Norman is really carrying and, in both cases, subtly reinforces the already established bird motif.

The **oblique** or **canted angle**, also called a **tilted shot**, is produced by shooting on a slant so the subject appears diagonal in the frame (see fig. 16). This shot usually suggests tension and trouble. Toward the end of *The 39 Steps* (1935), the hero Richard Hannay (Robert Donat), who has been following clues to discover a spy ring, realizes that the music hall performer, Mr. Memory, is the conduit of secret information. At Mr. Memory's performance, Hannay calls out, "What are 'The 39 Steps'?" An oblique angle on Mr. Memory visually conveys his tension, as he struggles between his compulsion to correctly answer the question and his fear of betraying the secret. *The Manchurian Candidate* provides other examples of the use of the oblique angle. In one case, just after Raymond has murdered his wife and father-in-law, Major Ben Marco (Frank Sinatra) returns home carrying a newspaper. A canted angle shows him entering the apartment, holding the newspaper with the headline on the murder clearly visible. The slanted framing conveys his feeling of distress and his guilt for not having stopped Raymond in time.

Camera angle is always affected by camera distance. A shot from close up will sharpen a high or low angle, and its dramatic quality will usually call attention to camera placement. The proximate distance alters the angle. Orson Welles is renowned for his use of extreme low-angle close-up shots. In *Citizen Kane*, for example, Kane's friend, Jedediah Leland (Joseph Cotten), comes into the newspaper office drunk after the election returns have come in. The camera is placed so low that Kane seems to overpower and dominate the frame. Here his power and domination are ironic, as Kane's election defeat has just been announced (see fig. 18).

Along with conveying or withholding information, camera angle almost always carries a certain emotional effect and often a judgment on the characters and situations. In *The Manchurian Candidate*, the audience sees Mrs. Iselin in a low angle and is repelled and frightened by her evil power over her son. In *Psycho*, the audience looks at the defenseless Arbogast from a high angle and is frightened for him. These intentional uses of camera angle provoke audience response.

The effect that camera angle can have on viewers watching a "real-life" televised event became apparent during the 1987 Iran-Contra hearings. An editorial in the June 21, 1987 issue of *The New Yorker* magazine pointed out that a TV camera was placed just below the witness table. For the viewers at home, the low-angle shot completely reversed the experience of the reporters physically present in the hearing room. For the reporters, witness Lieutenant-Colonel Oliver North was seated down low and the committee up high, in the usual positions of suspect and judges. But the low placement of the TV camera meant television viewers saw North from a low angle, which made him look like a movie hero—perhaps, in this case, like the image of a John Wayne doing his patriotic duty. The placement of a camera at a low angle created an effect favorable to North. Although under investigation and eventually indicted, for a time this witness became enough of a national hero to consider running for elective office. This set of circumstances proves once again the power of media representation.

Emotional meaning is usually presented by a **point-of-view** or **subjective** or **first-person shot**, so named because it presents a character's specific vantage point by showing the spectator what the character is look-

Figure 18. Citizen Kane. Jedediah Leland (Joseph Cotten) arrives in the newspaper office after Kane's defeat at the polls. The extreme low angle of the shot emphasizes Kane's dejection. Taken with a wide-angle lens, the shot achieves great depth of field, allowing all planes to remain in sharp focus at the same time.

ing at. In the past, these terms have been used interchangeably, but recently theorists have begun to distinguish differences among them. The **subjective shot** is sometimes considered a specific type of point-of-view shot that can also indicate a character's emotional, physical, or psychological state. In F.W. Murnau's *The Last Laugh* (1924), an aging hotel doorman suffers a hangover. As he struggles to get ready for work, the viewer sees through his eyes: objects are out of focus, distorted, and weaving (see fig. 46). Several other examples appear in Alfred Hitchcock's *Notorious* (1946). The morning after a drunken spree, Alicia (Ingrid Bergman) is seen lying in her bed. She opens her eyes and a subjective shot shows Devlin (Cary Grant) in an oblique angle, leaning on the door frame. He walks toward her and, at one point, appears to be approaching her upside down. At the end of the film, the subjective shot of Devlin approaching her is repeated, but this time Alicia's vision is distorted because of the effects of poison. The point-of-view shot is important in strategies of film storytelling.

■ Camera Movement

Decisions about the camera must be made. Should the shot remain fixed? Or would camera movement better serve the action and meaning of the shot? And if so, what kind of movement? The basic camera movements are panning, tracking, and the crane. Then the position of the camera—distance and angle—must be determined, nearly completing the setup. Lighting, the last element, is discussed in the next chapter.

In the **panning shot** or **pan** (from the word *panorama*), the camera is mounted on a stationary base and pivots on its axis. The camera moves along the line of the horizon from left to right or right to left. One of the simplest of camera movements, the pan is similar to a person looking to the left or to the right, while moving only her or his head.

A variation on the simple pan is the **swish pan**, which follows the same horizontal movement as the pan but so rapidly that the image blurs. In the breakfast montage scene of *Citizen Kane*, the camera moves quickly across the table from Kane to his wife during different phases of their marriage, suggesting the passage of time. Sometimes the swish pan is used as a transitional device to move the scene from one place to another or from one time period to another. A variation is the **tilt**, where a camera is mounted on a fixed base and moves either up or down instead of panning from side to side. In *Lone Star* (1995) John Sayles cleverly tilts the camera across the frame from Sam (Chris Cooper) to the object of his gaze, his girlfriend when they were teenagers, seamlessly making the transition from the present to the past, as the scene continues with the young couple.

In the **tracking shot**, also called a trucking or traveling shot, the camera films a subject while moving along with it. Originally it was called a tracking shot because the camera was mounted on a vehicle that moved along tracks laid on the set (see fig. 19). The movement increases the pace and allows the viewer to feel like a participant in the action. In *The Manchurian Candidate*, a single, continuous tracking shot (eventually revealed to be part of a dream) begins with a group of American soldiers seated on a stage (see fig. 20). Tracking slowly to the right, the camera passes across an audience of matrons listening to a garden club lecture. The camera continues tracking, seeming to move through a full circle. It passes the soldiers a second time, and ends on the stage where the lecturer has now become a Chinese scientist, speaking about brainwashing to a group of Russian and Chinese military officials. The effect is dramatic.

The camera can be mounted on a dolly, a vehicle specifically designed to allow flexible movement and equipped with rubber wheels allowing the camera to move freely while also cushioning the motion. In the **dolly shot**, the camera films while mounted on this miniaturized cart. When balloon wheels are used, smooth movement is produced that preserves the fluidity considered essential to professional-quality work. Because of its small size, the dolly can go into locations, especially interiors, where a larger mechanism such as the crane would not fit. Filmmakers working with small budgets have used everything from a tripod with wheels mounted on it to a supermarket cart to a wheelchair as they attempt to achieve the same results as a dolly.

In the **crane shot**, the cinematographer sits on a mechanical device that has a large telescoping arm on which the camera is attached. The crane allows the camera to move along a horizontal or vertical axis (see fig. 29). Since the 1930s, motorized cranes have permitted the camera to move freely in all directions so that complex camera movements can be created and action followed. Hitchcock arranged a dramatic crane shot in *Notorious* to mark a crucial point in the story. Alexander Sebastian (Claude Rains) is giving a party to introduce his bride, Alicia (Ingrid Bergman), to Rio de Janeiro's society. At the beginning of the sequence, the camera—mounted on a crane and located at the top of the mansion staircase—moves up into a high-angle extreme long shot of the foyer. From there, the camera slowly cranes downward, following the sweeping line of the staircase. The camera moves closer and closer to Alicia and Sebastian, who are standing near the front door greeting their guests, and the shot ends in an extreme close-up of Alicia's hand clutching the wine-cellar key that she had secreted earlier. The most striking aspect of the shot is that it moves from an extreme long shot to an extreme close-up without a cut, all in one fluid motion. Hitchcock stated, in an interview with Peter Bogdanovich in *The Cinema of Alfred Hitchcock*, that he wanted

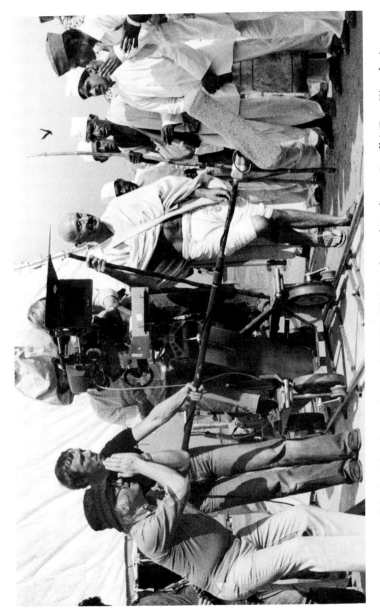

Figure 19. Gandhi (d. Richard Attenborough, 1982). This tracking shot shows Gandhi (Ben Kingsley) walking among his people. The camera accompanies him on tracks laid along his path. The resulting shot will be from Gandhi's point of view. The sound boom is held parallel to the tracks, out of camera range, while the director, at left, prompts the extras.

Figure 20. The Manchurian Candidate (d. John Frankenheimer, 1962).
Beginning with this long shot of a group of American soldiers (including Frank
Sinatra and Laurence Harvey) listening to a garden club lecture, the camera
slowly tracks to the right, seeming to move through a full circle, until it passes
the soldiers a second time and ends on the stage where the lecturer has
become a Chinese scientist speaking about brainwashing. Later this sequence
is revealed to be part of a dream.

to convey that a drama was quietly taking place in the midst of a large
and noisy party, a drama centered on a tiny key.

Professional motion picture cameras were so heavy that handheld
camera shots were nearly impossible. When filming with lightweight
cameras, a handheld shot tended to be choppy and, therefore, difficult to
watch. That limited the commercial use of this type of shot to those in-
frequent times when the filmmaker wanted the effect of uneven
movement. Handheld shots were more widely used by independent feature and documentary filmmakers, since they did not have access to
expensive, highly technical equipment. Eventually they came to appre-
ciate the freedom it gave them. Today mini-DV cameras can be held in
the palm of one's hand like a small still camera, allowing filmmakers to
be experimental and very discreet.

In 1959 two directors, Jean-Luc Godard and François Truffaut, who were among the founders of the French New Wave movement, used lightweight handheld cameras in their film debuts, *Breathless* and *The 400 Blows*. They did so partly because they could not afford expensive film equipment, but also because they wanted to rebel against the restrictive French studio system. They made a virtue of necessity and, putting their theories about film into practice, used the handheld camera as a way of marking their separateness from the dominant industry. Their theories led them to make films that called attention to the camera as well as to the act of filming.

The surprising success of the French New Wave and the flexibility of the mobile camera brought the technique to the attention of other filmmakers who were interested in exploring new methods. In his first feature film *Mean Streets* (1973), Martin Scorsese used a constantly moving handheld camera to follow Charlie (Harvey Keitel) through the maze of Little Italy. Many of the shots are nearly dizzying, as the camera tracks him through apartment hallways, into his nightclub hang-out, and along the neighborhood streets. They force the viewer to experience the mood of the action. In another example, the Italian director Gillo Pontecorvo used the handheld camera to achieve the look of a documentary in *The Battle of Algiers* (1966), which gives the effect of being in the middle of a crowd with the camera being jostled while filming.

■ Camera Speed

The camera can produce certain effects during the filming process by manipulating the lens or the speed of the filming. The most common effect is fast motion photography, where the camera films at a slower rate than the normal 24 frames per second. When the image is projected at normal speed, the action looks speeded up. Fast motion can be comical because of its slightly jerky, fast-paced quality. To achieve slow motion, the camera films at a faster rate than the normal speed. The action appears to slow down when the footage is projected at normal speed. Once reserved for dream sequences, director Arthur Penn found another application for slow motion in 1967 when he used four cameras running at different speeds to depict the deaths of Bonnie and Clyde. The shocking scene was so effective that showing graphic violence in slow motion became a convention. Today the technique has become a staple in the cinema of John Woo.

Ramping occurs when in-camera speeds shift during a single shot. In Peter Weir's *Fearless* (1993), the survivor of a catastrophic plane crash (Jeff Bridges) drifts in shock through a debris-strewn field. The camera hesitates as the magnitude of the disaster overwhelms the disoriented man, and then the camera speed accelerates as he snaps to his senses. Guy Ritchie's *Lock, Stock and Two Smoking Barrels* (1998) and *Snatch* (2001) use ramping to freeze characters in moments of extreme danger and then to accelerate again as they escape. The ramping technique suspends real time to place stylized emphasis on isolated moments, often reflecting a character's state of mind.

A variation of ramping called the "frozen moment" or "virtual dolly" gives the impression of a three-dimensional figure suspended in mid-action while a shot from a different perspective mimics a camera dolly move. In Matthew Rolston's Gap commercial "Khaki Swing" (1998), dancers jump and freeze in mid-air as the camera sweeps around them. A rig was mounted with 150 cameras programmed to snap still images from different angles. These images were later animated in postproduction to form one continuous shot. Larry and Andy Wachowski use a similar technique, which they call "bullet time," in *The Matrix*. As Neo (Keanu Reeves) and his opponents leap through the air, guns blazing, the camera tracks around them after slowing down to the point where the characters seem motionless and their bullets become visible. Although the action never freezes, the innovative effect resembles the virtual dolly. Commercials and music videos inspire directors to experiment with new forms of film language.

■ Optical Processes

Filmmaking once required the services of a laboratory for processing exposed film, producing effects, and making release prints. To provide these services, lab technicians used different types of **optical printers**, automated camera-and-projector combinations. Many optical processes are now done digitally.

The most common optical processes, the fade-out and fade-in, can be attained in the camera itself. In a **fade-out**, the camera's variable shutter is gradually closed down so the image gradually darkens from normal brightness to black. The fade-out almost always marks the end of a sequence. Occasionally the fade is to another color, for example, to white in Mike Nichols's *Catch-22* (1970) or to red in Ingmar Bergman's *Cries and Whispers* (1972). During a **fade-in**, the variable shutter is gradually opened, so the image gradually appears from a black screen. The fade-in usually marks the beginning of a sequence. Although these transitional devices can be done in the camera, professional filmmakers rely on the lab or digital editing systems to produce them in the postproduction phase of filmmaking.

In a **dissolve**, also called a lap dissolve from the term *overlapping dissolve*, one image begins to disappear as another begins to surface. At some point two images are superimposed upon each other (see fig. 21). The speed of the dissolve can be timed in the laboratory. Very fast dissolves are sometimes used to smooth a cut and are scarcely detectable to the viewer. Long, slow dissolves emphasize the association between images. In classic films, dream sequences and flashbacks are almost always introduced by dissolves. *The Manchurian Candidate* uses the dissolve in both of these narrative situations. Major Marco's nightmare begins with a gradual dissolve from his face to his dream and ends with a close-up on his face, which dissolves quickly to him waking up. Another sequence dissolves into Lieutenant Melvin's nearly identical nightmare, an African-American version of Marco's bad dream with blacks in the appropriate key roles. Later Raymond Shaw tells Marco the story of his meeting and summer romance with Jocelyn Jordan; a long, languid dissolve keeps Shaw on the screen telling the story, as the story's scene comes up slowly in the background and then takes over the screen.

The **iris** is a type of masking device that blocks out or masks part of the picture, while another part, usually in the shape of a circle or oval, contains the visible image. Irising in and irising out describe the contrac-

*Figure 21. **The Gold Rush*** (d. Charlie Chaplin, 1925). A dissolve turns the Little Tramp (Charlie Chaplin) into a chicken. This subjective shot represents the point of view of Big Jim McKay, the Tramp's partner. Trapped by a snowstorm and starving, McKay begins to hallucinate and sees a fine meal just out of reach.

tion and expansion of the image. The technique visually emphasizes a particular area of the frame by closing in on it and then opening to show its relation to the larger setting. Commonly used in early silent films, the iris virtually disappeared by the advent of sound.

A **freeze frame** or **freeze** is another laboratory optical process in which a single frame is reprinted many times so that it looks like a still photograph when projected; the action appears to have stopped. In the final shot of Truffaut's *The 400 Blows*, the young protagonist (Jean-Pierre Leaud) runs toward the ocean, and, as he turns back toward the camera, the shot traps him in a freeze frame that lends ambiguity to the ending.

The developing and color timing of a film-to-film answer print still occur in the lab. Attaining precision and saturation with color, particularly black, requires meticulous work. A costly silver-retention process called the bleach-bypass method produces a truer, deeper level of black in such movies as David Fincher's *The Game* (1997). On the other hand, color and contrast changes are easy to achieve during the telecine process, the transfer of film to videotape for broadcast formats. A colorist can make adjustments to color, light, and contrast with a keystroke—experimenting easily and repeatedly with various looks.

■ Special Effects

Special effects work is the art of the fantastic. A **special effect** (**FX**) is any technique or device that creates an illusion of reality in a situation where it is not possible, safe, or economical to achieve the same result with conventional cinematography. Through advances in visual technology—physical, photographic or optical, digital—a wide variety of images can be manipulated, making possible almost anything imaginable.

In the late 1970s and early 1980s, a digital revolution began when the *Star Wars* trilogy, *E.T.*, *Blade Runner*, and later both *Terminator* movies generated a great deal of attention and profits. Then in 1993, digital tools created the *Jurassic Park* dinosaurs. From the gentle, giraffe-like Brachiosaurus nibbling a tree top to seven-foot-high Velociraptors stalking terrified children, these dinosaurs have the fluidity of movement and appearance of living creatures. The entire world took notice of the first film to use computers as the main device for creating characters. As a result of the tremendous box-office success of these movies, the studios began to produce more special effects-driven blockbusters, even though their production and distribution costs were extremely high.

James Cameron's *Titanic*, produced in 1997 for $200 million, could not have recreated the legendary 1912 maritime disaster without computer-generated imagery. In the stunning climax, the ship splits in half, its stern tilting upwards while desperate passengers cling to the suddenly perpendicular deck or plummet from its heights into the icy water. The film's tremendous earnings encouraged the financing of more spectacles featuring complex visual effects, such as *Pearl Harbor* (2001). Blockbusters have become an industry staple. Yet digital effects work is common in all film and television productions, including music videos and commercials. Digital Domain, Industrial Light & Magic (ILM), and Pacific Data Images (PDI) are in great demand for their expertise in creating state-of-the-art digital effects.

Because of the increasingly sophisticated production of fantastic creatures, landscapes, machinery, natural disasters, and other stunning visuals that suggest a bygone era or a distant future, viewers may be tempted to think of special effects as a recent phenomenon. Actually special effects go back to the beginning of the film business. **Stop-motion photography**, also called single frame or stop-action photography, creates the illusion that an inanimate object can move on its own. The camera exposes one frame at a time, and the position of the object or person is changed between shots. When the footage is projected, the illusion of continuous movement makes the special effects sequence seem realistic. In 1902 film pioneer Georges Méliès used stop-motion photography to make moon creatures disappear when scientists hit them with umbrellas in *A Trip to the Moon*. Early special effects designer Willis O'Brien relied on the same technique to make his model of King Kong come alive in 1933. Stop-motion photography of models and miniatures, paintings and drawings, and make-up effects provided the foundation for early fantasy, horror, and science fiction films.

Due to advancements in computer technology, significant refinements of stop-motion photography took place in the 1970s. **Go-motion** refers to animated miniatures under electronic control, which allows them to be in motion while the camera shutter is open. This technique causes a natural blur of motion that adds realism to the shot. Most important was the development of computer-controlled servomotors that make **motion control photography** possible. This system programs the camera to repeat elaborate moves precisely and at any speed, enabling filmmakers to shoot pass after pass of the same action. Each pass contains a different image or element, and later all passes are composited in an optical printer. Recall part of the exciting climax of *Star Wars* in which Darth Vader's T.I.E. fighter pursues and fires at Luke Skywalker's X-Wing as they race across the surface of the Death Star. A single effects shot in this scene combined many elements, each filmed separately against blue screen and each repeating the same movement away from the camera: Vader's T.I.E. fighter, Luke's X-Wing fighter, an animated laser blast, footage of the trench across the surface of the Death Star, and a star field beyond it. Because of motion control photography, the space battle is as thrilling and realistic as a live-action dogfight, and much safer.

Developed in 1932, the principle of **composite photography** combines two or more images on a single negative so they appear to be photographed together. **Rear projection** or **process photography** combines live action taking place in the foreground with a moving background, usually scenery, projected onto a translucent screen behind the actors. With this technique, backgrounds can be provided without actually shooting on location or endangering actors. Hitchcock used rear projection extensively, especially in many scenes where characters are driving in automobiles against picturesque and recognizable locations. *Vertigo, Notorious*, and *To Catch a Thief* include scenes using rear projection to provide backgrounds of Northern California, Florida, and the French Riviera, respectively. In *North by Northwest* Cary Grant runs across an open field, partially recreated on a sound stage at MGM, while a crop duster swoops behind him on a rear-projection screen.

Some composite processes are controlled in the laboratory by the use of the optical printer. The **matte shot** prints two separate shots onto a single piece of film stock, resulting in a single image. The **traveling matte** process allows composites to be produced in which moving material is combined with backgrounds shot elsewhere. This technique placed Fay Wray and the gorilla together in the same frame of *King Kong*. **Blue-screen** and **green-screen photography** are traveling matte systems that depend upon the way color film stocks respond to different wavelengths of light. Foreground elements such as actors can be filmed in front of a brightly illuminated blue or green screen that can be optically erased. Then the image can be combined with background shots filmed elsewhere.

Contemporary special effects artists generally use computer workstations—not optical printers—to matte and composite digital images. **Compositing** can build multiple layers of digital images, and each layer can be independently manipulated, removed, altered, and replaced with no loss of resolution. This digital technique allowed Tom Hanks, playing the fictional hero of *Forrest Gump* (1994), to shake hands with the real John F. Kennedy.

Most traditional techniques have been supplemented, if not supplanted, by **computer-generated imagery** (**CGI** or **CG**) that offers spectacular and cost-effective results. With improvements in resolution and the degree of manipulation allowed by computers, the new technology has become an essential tool of both artists and technicians. A filmmaker can shoot a scene on film or digital video, scan or import it into a computer, manipulate the data, and then output the altered images to film, video, multimedia, or the Web.

Morphing (from the word *metamorphosis*) is a commonplace three-dimensional, shape-changing effect in which digital image processing transforms one figure smoothly into another. Although *Willow* (1988) was the first feature film to use this effect, filmgoers really took notice later, charmed by the shimmering water snake in *The Abyss* (1989) and fascinated by the T-1000 android villain who changes back and forth from human to liquid-metal forms in *Terminator 2: Judgment Day* (1991). Michael Jackson's *Black or White* music video and the Exxon commercial that converted a car into a running tiger introduced morphing to television audiences (see fig. 22).

Two-dimensional digital applications, such as wire and rig removal, once comprised the bulk of CGI work. In *Terminator 2*, Arnold Schwarzenegger appears to fly through the air on his motorcycle in a jump scene. In fact he was suspended by wires that were removed digitally and replaced by data representing blue sky. Reality-based effects include touching up the crow's feet around an actor's eyes, changing brown grass to green, or "cloning" extras and adding them to a set (see fig. 23).

Individuals who can handle both filmmaking and pixels are determining the way movies are planned, shot, edited, composited, and shown to an increasingly discerning public. John Lassiter directed the first fully computer-animated feature film, *Toy Story* (1995). Digital technology functioned as a tool to bring the film's lovable characters and good storytelling to the screen, thus combining computer skills and traditional Hollywood methods. The same can be said about director Lynn Hershman Leeson's *Conceiving Ada* (1997), the story of the "mother of all computer programmers" Ada Byron King. Using the very technology that Byron King pioneered, Hershman Leeson made the first feature that laid down still images onto digital videotape—lush virtual sets—while the actors performed before a monitor showing them their environment (see figure 24). This innovative technical breakthrough allowed Hershman Leeson to produce a complex piece set during the present and the Victorian era for a fraction of the usual set construction and location costs, and allowed the actors to deliver a more believable performance than if they had performed before a blue screen with no sense of their surroundings.

No wonder actors worry that filmmakers might eventually eliminate them from the moviemaking process, replacing their images and high-priced salary demands with digitized performers. The photo-realist human beings in Hironobu Sakaguchi's *Final Fantasy: The Spirits Within* (2001), particularly heroine Aki Ross (voiced by Ming-Na), open a new realm of possibilities; more than 200 artists from 22 countries worked for over three years to complete this animated imitation of life. Some special effects artists, too, are concerned CGI will make traditional methods obsolete. Yet model work—including miniatures, puppetry and animatronics—is one discipline essential to the creation of digital effects.

A

B

C

Figure 22 A-C. Computer-generated effects (CGI or CG), such as this morphing sequence by Pacific Data Images (PDI), are changing the production methods and looks of film, television, and advertising.

(Exxon *You Know*)

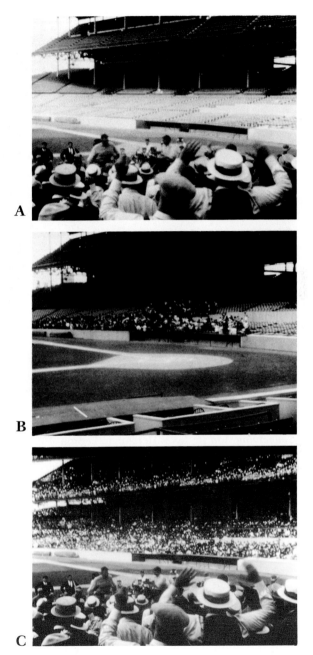

Figure 23 A-C. The Babe (d. Arthur Hiller, 1992). By producing reality-based effects through digital image processing and compositing techniques, Pacific Data Images (PDI) was able to add historical details and still cut production costs. PDI digitally constructed a second deck for the minor league ballpark used as a location (A) and "cloned" a small group of extras (B), combining both images to create an authentic stadium full of baseball fans (C).

(Universal Studios *The Babe*)

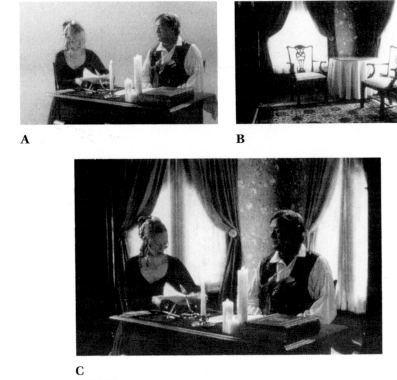

A   B

C

Figure 24 A-C. Conceiving Ada (d. Lynn Hershman Leeson, 1997). For this work, the filmmaker designed a special technical process that allows digital background images to be manipulated and placed into live video. Actors Tilda Swinton and Owen Murphy sit at a real table in front of a blue screen (A). While they performed before a monitor showing them their virtual surroundings, a computer-generated Victorian set (B), digital videotape recorded in real time their live-action images and the well-appointed room (C).

(Photograph by Mark Garrett. Courtesy of Lynn Hershman Leeson, © 1997)

When filmmakers start to fashion narratives and bring characters to life that could not be created any other way, a marriage between story and special effects takes place. The artistry of these techniques makes it difficult for viewers to see the effects because even the most fantastic ones look so real. From the vivid imaginary worlds of *Star Wars* to the lush Victorian interiors of *Conceiving Ada* to the reenacted sinking of the ocean liner *Titanic* or the bombing of *Pearl Harbor*, special effects work is movie magic. But the best filmmakers know that technology is simply a tool to support the story and that visual effects can only help make better-looking movies, not better ones.

Chapter 4

Mise en Scène

Mise en scène (pronounced "meez on sen") is a French term, which translated means placement into the scene or, in everyday English, "setting the scene." **Mise en scène** refers to everything put in front of the camera in preparation for filming. This includes sets and locations, props and objects, costuming, color design, actors and acting, blocking and choreography, and lighting. The director and cinematographer's choices in these areas, as well as their selection of film stock or videotape, lenses, camera angles, and camera distances, determine the way the filmed images actually look and that, in turn, affects the viewer's reading of the *mise en scène*. All of the following elements must be managed by the director in the course of making a movie.

■ Sets and Locations

Sets are the "little worlds" created in the production studio for feature films (see fig. 25). Even before a final shooting script has been completed, the director works with the production designer to plan the requirements of the set. After researching decor and architecture, the production designer is responsible for illustrations and sketches of each scene. In order to create authentic and acceptable backdrops, the production designer supervises scenic artists, light and color specialists, and the costume designer. Studios often use sound stages, large spaces designed for good acoustics and good lighting, in which the production designer plans and constructs decors. A sound stage requires the labor of carpenters, metal workers, painters, electricians, and decorators. A commercially-produced feature may use fifty to two hundred skilled craftspersons; technical and

Figure 25. How Green Was My Valley (d. John Ford, 1941). This set is a "little world" that romanticizes a Welsh coal-mining village on Twentieth Century-Fox's studio backlot.

artistic advisers are also consulted to ensure authenticity. Some studios own backlots where special exteriors can be fabricated, such as a town of the Old West. The set is a physical space marked out for the movements of both actors and camera. The actors must move naturally in the area, and the camera must be free to pass from room to room, climb stairs, circle in a ballroom, hover high above the scene, or take the place of characters within the action.

Locations are actual places chosen as the backdrop for the action. They are natural settings and cannot be controlled like a specially constructed set. Elements inappropriate to a movie, such as electric power lines in an eighteenth-century setting, must be eliminated so they do not undermine the film's believability. Yet shooting on location is desirable for realism. Since the development of lightweight sound cameras, tape recorders, and lighting equipment, directors of feature films "take to the hills" as well as to the streets whenever they wish.

Genre films, especially adventure stories and Westerns, require natural settings and are almost always filmed at least partly on location, on the Hollywood backlots, or in places such as Monument Valley, Utah, or Lone Pine in eastern California. Narrative development depends on location and props. Imagine a situation in which the hero is being chased by villains. Put the characters on horses in a wilderness setting, give them rifles, and you have a Western (*The Searchers*, 1956; *Unforgiven*, 1992). Put them into low-slung automobiles in an urban setting, give them machine guns and .38s, and you have a gangster movie (*Scarface*, 1932; *The Untouchables*, 1987). Put them in a spaceship, give them light sabers, and you have, of course, science fiction (*Star Wars*, 1977).

The setting must fulfill the essential needs of the production by providing the scenery necessary to the story—from the landscape to the buildings, their decor, and furnishings. Usually filmmakers need to modify or transform natural locations for purposes of story and style. With imagination and hard work, a production designer can change a physical backdrop into one of the most essential elements of a film. To capture Ridley Scott's dark vision of the future in *Blade Runner* (1982), production designer Lawrence Paull supervised two storyboard artists, an art director, and a "visual futurist." Some scenes were shot on location in front of the Bradbury Building in downtown Los Angeles, where the crew "dressed" the real street by placing litter and debris everywhere to suggest urban decay in the year 2019. Most of the sets, however, were constructed on backlots and in sound stages at the Warner Brothers studio facility in Burbank, California. Extensive special effects using miniatures and matte paintings produced the aerial views of the fictional Tyrell Corporation headquarters with the surrounding vast industrial wasteland. The extraordinary result was a labyrinth of gigantic electronic billboards, squalid, narrow, overcrowded streets, dank warehouses, and

Figure 26. Blade Runner (d. Ridley Scott, 1982). The production designer and his crew constructed this set on a Warner Brothers backlot, creating everything from the neon signs to the futuristic vehicles. Against the physical backdrop of urban decay in the year 2019, Deckard (Harrison Ford) searches for a replicant. (BLADERUNNER © 1982 The Bladerunner Partnership. All Rights Reserved.)

over-sized skyscrapers that evokes the oppressive and claustrophobic mood (see fig. 26).

Locations are carefully chosen for the look and feel of the place and to contribute to the meaning of the film. Alfred Hitchcock filmed *Vertigo* in San Francisco and the surrounding Bay Area. He deliberately set out to demonstrate that bright daylight, stunning views, natural landscapes, and a pastel-colored city could conceal murder, deceit, corruption, and despair as effectively as the harsh urban settings used in the thrillers known as *film noir*. For *Mishima* (1985), Paul Schrader used detailed and expressionistic sets intercut with everyday, realistic scenes to make a statement about the writer-philosopher Yukio Mishima's complex psychology, while at the same time conveying the visual equivalent of the writer's stylized fiction (see fig. 34). Films cannot exist without sets or locations, either real or created, and the best films use the physical world to convey more than time period and place.

■ Props and Objects

The choice and placement of **props**—furnishings, objects of art, decoration, all the various pertinent objects related to the scene and story—support the authenticity of the setting and add meaning to the film. In *Blade Runner* everything was specially designed: neon signs, telephones, furniture, even the newspapers. Los Angeles of the future is depicted as a bloated, decaying megalopolis, so rather than making the futuristic props hi-tech and shiny, everything looks deteriorated and recycled, patched and repaired.

A prop can also have strongly symbolic overtones. In Alfred Hitchcock's *Psycho*, the large stuffed owl in the parlor of the Bates Motel, beneath which Norman (Anthony Perkins) stands after his conversation with Marion Crane (Janet Leigh), serves a dual function: as a simple prop, the owl demonstrates Norman's decorating taste and taxidermy skills (the extent and implications of which are later revealed), and yet it also symbolizes his own predatory nature.

■ Costuming

The costume designer is responsible for what the actors wear. **Costumes**, which include all apparel and accessories, have an important place in defining character (see fig. 27). Clothes always indicate a character's social class and sense of style. A costume also can assume symbolic overtones. In early Westerns, the good guys always wore white hats, and the villains always wore black ones. The cold-blooded women in *film noir*, *femmes fatales* who seduce and then betray the men, are often dressed in

Figure 27. *Casablanca* (d. Michael Curtiz, 1942). Costumes help establish the authenticity of location and period. Because of the dark color of Captain Reynaud's (Claude Rains) uniform, the viewer's eye is drawn to him. He stands protectively between the French soldier and Victor (Paul Henreid), Rick (Humphrey Bogart), and Ilsa (Ingrid Bergman), all dressed in the light colors associated with the hero.

sequins and satin or feathers and fur to associate them with the mysterious and wild animal world. When fashioning costumes, a designer must ensure that the characters are appropriately dressed for the period of the story. Because texture and colors photograph differently, the costume designer must also consider every detail of the wardrobe both in terms of its look on screen and its place in the film's overall production design.

■ Color Design

The set, costuming, and lighting contribute to the color design of a film. Because color comes from a number of sources, collaboration among the director, cinematographer, production and costume designers is essential in controlling the total effect. Color film flattens the image, decreasing the sense of depth. Color may also be a distraction. Bright hues such as red, yellow, and orange tend to attract the viewer's attention. Careful control of the color design prevents insignificant characters or objects from standing out, thus disturbing the balance and meaning of the shot.

Color design can be used dramatically or to express thematic ideas, emotional moods, and psychological states In his first color film, *Red Desert* (1964), Michelangelo Antonioni experimented with distorting natural colors to produce an unnatural world, an effect meant to reflect the main character's mental anguish. He had the fruit at a street vendor's stand tinted gray, a waterfront shack painted a brilliant red, and yellow smoke blown from a factory chimney. The harsh primary colors, contrasted against the grayed-down ones of the rest of the scene, represent the character's intense anxiety in contemporary industrial society. In *Drugstore Cowboy* (1989), director Gus Van Sant makes the colors much more vivid once the main character (Matt Dillon) gives up drugs and gains a clear-eyed view of life around him.

Steven Soderbergh's *Traffic* (2000) has three distinct visual looks, a different color design for each narrative thread. The first story strand follows a pair of Mexican policemen (Benicio Del Toro and Jacob Vargas) caught between two drug cartels. All the scenes set in Mexico have an overexposed, yellowish-brown look that was achieved through a combination of techniques, including the use of "tobacco" filters and extensive lab work. In the second story, a newly appointed Washington drug czar (Michael Douglas) reconsiders the national drug policy when his teenager (Erika Christensen) becomes a junkie. A cool blue tint sets the tone for the East Coast complications of the plot. In the third story, the wife (Catherine Zeta-Jones) of an arrested San Diego drug smuggler (Steven Bauer) takes charge of his lucrative business and transforms from a country club charmer to one of the most ruthless characters in the film. These images look soft and bright in counterpoint to the ugly underpinnings of the couple's lifestyle. The color design helps viewers keep track of the multiple plotlines and numerous characters, signaling a change in location before anyone enters the scene.

■ Actors and Acting

Because of the physical presence of the camera on the set with the actors, and because performances are photographed for a few minutes at a time, film acting is technically more complex than stage acting where performances take place in a continuous time period in front of an audience. Movies consist of many different scenes, each of which must be acted separately. Films are not shot in the chronological order of the story but according to factors such as time of day, season, place of action (interiors, exteriors, on location, on a studio set), equipment availability, or actors' schedules. Film actors may not have to memorize lines for a two-hour performance like their theatrical counterparts, but they do have to step into their roles without an audience to play to every time there is a new take.

Film acting, then, differs from acting in the theater. Whereas stage acting is expansive and broad, screen acting is subtle. The reason for the difference is fairly obvious: in the theater, the audience is always relatively far away from the actors who must project their voice, gestures, and actions so that all the spectators, whether seated in the first row of the orchestra or the last row of the balcony, can understand the play. Once film directors realized the camera could move, they understood that a close-up would intensify even the most understated emotions. The slightest tightening around the lips, a glance, the slow clenching of a fist or stiffening of the shoulders, magnified by the close-up, expressed meaning and emotion even more powerfully than did a grand gesture.

A naturalistic style of acting became the norm in American films during the 1930s and 1940s, partly because the studios cast actors in roles that showcased their personalities and tailored scripts to their special talents. Valuable star properties like Clark Gable and Bette Davis were competent professional actors who used theater-based techniques, including a reliance on props and voice, to reveal character. But they seldom varied their film performances and often relied on the same characteristics, gestures, and personal mannerisms in every role. Gable's smile and Davis's hand gesture, for instance, became trademarks to movie audiences.

While the star system has changed since the studio years, and although some directors also have marquee value, the movies are still most associated with stars. They are the celebrities that elicit the greatest audience response. Audience recognition and response guarantee box office receipts and, therefore, drive production.

A star can "make" a picture. That is, a star attached to a production helps it obtain financing and increases its chances for box-office success. Just as advertising sells products through brand recognition, so does a movie depend on the recognition of a brand name: the movie star. People go to a "Russell Crowe" or a "Chow Yun-fat" film, or see everything that Julia Roberts or Jennifer Lopez has made. These stars are bankable. Although a star cannot make a bad movie work, he or she can "open" a film and help it make money during the crucial first weekend of release.

The **star image**, the combination of an actor's screen and real-life persona, was carefully manufactured and controlled in the Golden Age by studio publicity departments to endear the star to the viewing public. Today publicists and agencies hired by the stars, as well as the film and television studios, try to promote them and encourage the support of loyal fans.

Screen actors have always been chosen for their look, as much as for their looks. This is called **iconography**, the likeness or image of the actor that produces a particular meaning (see fig. 28). One of the best known actors ever to come out of the star system, John Wayne is inseparable from the roles he played. He represents a specific range of meanings and connotations: independence, individuality, courage, integrity, and rugged masculinity. Among contemporary actors, Susan Sarandon combines the requirements of feminine good looks with independence, strength of character, and resourcefulness in *Bull Durham* (1988), *Thelma and Louise* (1992), and *Dead Man Walking* (1995).

Motion picture acting was revolutionized when Method acting was brought from the theater to the screen by Marlon Brando, who stunned Hollywood with his performance in *A Streetcar Named Desire* (1951) and *On the Waterfront* (1954). Developed by Elia Kazan and Lee Strasberg at the Actors Studio in New York, **Method acting** stressed "being" the character over "acting" roles and memorizing lines. Actors were encouraged to become personally involved in their roles by seeking experiences equivalent to those of their characters—either through emotive memory, that is, drawing on emotions derived from personal experience, or through keen observation. The training emphasized improvisation. Robert De Niro, a disciple of the Method school of acting, prepared himself for his parts

Figure 28. The Left-Handed Gun (d. Arthur Penn, 1958). Paul Newman's strong, unwavering gaze is characteristic of the iconography of the Western hero.

(© Warner Bros. Pictures, Inc.)

by driving a cab in *Taxi Driver* (1976), hanging around with steelworkers in Pennsylvania bars for *The Deer Hunter* (1978), and gaining over fifty pounds to transform himself into the has-been boxer, Jake La Motta, for *Raging Bull* (1980). This "put-yourself-into-their-shoes" approach to screen acting inspires the actor to "become" the character and allows a dedicated actor to explore human psychology and deliver a realistic, subtly nuanced performance. The Method elevated film acting from a craft to an art form in which the actor contributes creatively to the film.

■ Blocking and Choreography

Actors interact not only with each other but also with a camera that is usually moving. The director diagrams the **blocking**, the movements of both actors and camera, to bring both to the right place at precisely the right time, so the actors "hit the mark," the spot where they will be in focus and correctly lit. Descriptions of the filming of Alfred Hitchcock's *Under Capricorn* (1949) illustrate the difficulties involved. The takes were nearly ten minutes long, and the camera was in constant motion, mov-

Figure 29. Director Victor Fleming blocks and choreographs the action for a crane shot during the making of *Gone With the Wind* (1939).

ing about the set, dollying in for a close-up on one actor, then circling away to concentrate on another. The performers were also constantly moving and had to arrive at their places marked on the floor at the exact moment that they were to be filmed. The slightest lapse in timing or a missed mark meant redoing the entire take. Ingrid Bergman, the star, was said to have broken down under the stress of this very demanding requirement.

Blocking and **choreography** are both terms for plotting the movements of actors and camera. The director and the production designer must be able to visualize the movements of actors as they interact with the camera. They also must be able to create a set not for just a couple of shots but for the whole film (see fig. 29). Alfred Hitchcock's *Rope* (1948) was shot in a single location with hardly any detectable cutting. The camera followed the actors through a set that represented a single room in a New York penthouse but was made up of at least three spaces. It was the production designer's job to make sure that the decor in all three rooms connected, that they worked together as one, and that there was sufficient space to block out movement.

For *The Magnificent Ambersons* (1942), Orson Welles demanded the creation of a very elaborate set to represent an opulent nineteenth century mansion belonging to a wealthy family. The ballroom sequence alone required space ample enough for the camera and the two dancing couples to move and interact in relation to one another (see fig. 12).

■ Lighting

Subtle variations in lighting create mood and atmosphere. Whether a film production is on a set or on location, the cinematographer or director of photography spends many hours on the lighting design. Choices must be made about the intensity, character, and direction of the light. The decisions take a considerable amount of time to implement but contribute greatly to a scene's dramatic effectiveness. A skilled crew of lighting technicians called gaffers adjust the lights. They work under the supervision of the cinematographer, whose extensive technical knowledge makes it possible to achieve the visual look asked for by the director.

Lighting technique consists of working with the contrast ratio between darker and lighter portions of the set. Film stocks have different tolerances for contrast, so the cinematographer has to be sure that the range between the darkest and lightest areas of the set or location is not too extreme for the film type being used. Then the cinematographer, working with lights of varying intensities, models the scene to emphasize the facial characteristics of the actors or the shape of objects and to most effectively convey the meaning that the director intends to establish through the shot. For example, Josef von Sternberg insisted on lighting his star,

Figure 30. Seven Sinners (d. Tay Garnett, 1940). To emphasize Marlene Dietrich's bone structure, directors such as Josef von Sternberg and Tay Garnett insisted on lighting that modeled her face. (Copyright ® by Universal Studios, Inc. Courtesy of MCA Publishing Rights, a Division of MCA Inc.)

Marlene Dietrich, in such a way that it modeled her face to emphasize her bone structure (see fig. 30).

In his book, *Thinking In Pictures*, independent filmmaker John Sayles describes the lighting strategy of his film *Matewan* (1987). For this story of coal miners in the 1920s, Sayles and cinematographer Haskell Wexler wanted to avoid conventional lighting setups for the shots inside the mines. Miners at the time worked using low-intensity carbide headlamps, inadequate for filming. Sayles wanted the scenes to show the real darkness in which the miners worked, but their activities had to be visible on the screen. Wexler solved the problem by setting up a diffuse spotlight. He carefully aimed the light past the miner without focusing on any one place and synchronized it with the movement of the miner's head so that it appeared to be coming from the headlamp. The setup was so complex that the least slip in timing would ruin the shot.

The single light setup used for *Matewan* is rare, as most productions use many lights. A basic lighting setup involves two lights: a key light and a fill light. The **key light** is the primary or key source of illumination. A **fill light** is softer, diffuse, and of lower intensity than the key. It reduces the contrast between the light and dark areas of the frame by filling in and balancing the shadows. A **backlight**, as the name suggests, can be placed behind the subject to separate it from the background. While not part of the basic setup, **bounce lighting** reflects or bounces intense light off a bright white wall or a metallic reflector to reduce the strength of a light source and diffuse it over the area to be photographed. Other optional lights are **hairlights**, which get their name from being placed high behind the subject to illuminate the hair and the back of the head, creating a halo effect. **Kickers**, placed near the feet at floor level, are aimed upward and also serve to separate subject from background.

Whether a scene is illuminated naturally by sunlight or artificially by incandescent bulbs, quartz lights, or xenon arc lamps, the character of the light is very important. The character of natural light, for instance, may vary greatly depending on the time of day or whether the sky is clear, hazy, or cloudy. John Ford preferred to shoot his Westerns in the late afternoon sunlight due to its warmer red tones and the long shadows cast. Silk and metal screens and reflectors can further affect the character of outdoor light by softening or redirecting the rays of the sun. Artificial light also has different qualities. The focused beam of a spotlight is usually harsh in character, whereas a floodlight is soft and diffuse. Such choices modify the look of the image, which, in turn, produces meaning.

The direction of the light plays an important role in the dramatic effectiveness of an image. Front, overhead, back and side lighting create entirely different results. A romantic heroine may look angelic if backlighting produces a "halo" around her head. A villain may appear psychotic if strong side lighting illuminates only half of his face, keeping his "dark" side in blackness. If lit from below, a monster may seem even more threatening because of the grotesque shadows cast on its face. In less striking examples, the subject may simply appear normal, even though there is nothing simple or normal about any lighting assignment.

Different styles of lighting serve different purposes. **High-key lighting** uses a strong primary light source with a great deal of fill light to create

Figure 31. Strong contrasts between light and shadow are typical of the thriller and *film noir*. In an interview published in *Focus on Hitchcock*, the director talked about working against the convention captured in the above picture: the protagonist "under the street lamp at night in a pool of light, waiting, very sinister surroundings, the cobbles are all washed by the recent rain . . ."

bright, even illumination. It establishes an upbeat tone suitable for comedies and musicals. **Low-key lighting** creates scenes of **high contrast**, which contain a wide range of light and dark areas. Rich, black shadows and atmospheric pools of light are produced by using a strong primary light source and very little fill light. The grim, tough, detective films and thrillers of the late 1940s were called *film noir*, which seemed appropriate because the black-and-white photography captured harsh, high-contrast images lit in a low-key style that expressed the films' dark and somber themes. In the *noir* films (including, among others, *Double Indemnity*, 1944; *The Big Sleep*, 1946; *The Postman Always Rings Twice*, 1946; *Out of the Past*, 1947), the dramatic lighting conceals the hidden dangers of a corrupt and violent world and establishes a bleak, pessimistic mood (see figs. 31, 32, 33).

The cinematographer and the director make decisions on lighting according to the demands of the particular project, knowing that the lighting affects both the quality of the image and the production of meaning. Vittorio Storaro (*The Conformist*, 1970; *Apocalypse Now*, 1979; *The Last*

Figure 32. Double Indemnity (d. Billy Wilder, 1944). Fred McMurray and Barbara Stanwyck discuss "insurance" in a room full of shadows and pools of light. A classic example of *film noir* cinematography, the low-key lighting style establishes the film's mood and reflects the dark themes of corruption and despair.

Figure 33. *The Postman Always Rings Twice* (d. Tay Garnett, 1946). The light casts shadows of the unseen cell bars, emphasizing the idea of a moral and physical cage in which this man is trapped. Typical of *film noir*, the mood of the lighting is bleak and despairing.

Emperor, 1987) said in an interview that he considers the cinematographer to be like a writer and filming to be like writing with light, enabling the viewer to feel and understand, both consciously and unconsciously, the meaning of the story.

If the lighting is not flamboyant or dramatic or striking, it will not be noticed at all—as lighting. The drive for realism, even in nonrealistic genres like science fiction, has restricted experimentation and any obvious manipulation of lighting. Often the cinematographer's art is an invisible one, yet it influences the meaning of the film.

■ Composition

Whereas the notion of *mise en scène* originated in the theater, the concept of **composition** pertains to the visual arts where it refers to the deliberate organization of any work. In painting and photography, composition is defined as the arrangement of the parts of a work to form a

Figure 34. Mishima (d. Paul Schrader, 1985). A careful balance of the figures and the stylized set into which they are placed emphasizes the depth of the frame, all the way to the vanishing point, which is blocked by the main figure facing forward. The horizon line and the sweep of the clouds give greater depth to the frame in this example of linear perspective.

unified, harmonious whole. Studies in the psychology of perception have shown that viewers try to find harmony and balance in visual compositions; if they cannot, they feel anxiety and tension. Like painters and other visual artists, filmmakers can manipulate composition to emphasize harmony or disharmony to produce response within the viewer.

Composition in film establishes a relationship among all the elements of the *mise en scène*. The choices made by the director and cinematographer in the arrangement of visual elements within the frame come from aesthetic traditions that, in European-influenced cultures, date back to the Renaissance and specifically to principles of classical composition in art. Although there are many complex issues to consider, the principles

Figure 35. *Letter from an Unknown Woman* (d. Max Ophuls, 1947). The line of snow running at a diagonal in the middleground marks a division between the foreground in sharp focus and the background in soft focus and soft grays. This is an example of aerial perspective that gives depth to the frame.

of composition defined in this chapter are those that have dominated Western film tradition since its inception. They provide the basis for the examination and analysis of films.

Since the Renaissance, perspective has been a fundamental principle of Western conceptions of the image. **Perspective** creates the illusion of three-dimensional space on a two-dimensional surface. Various techniques are used to create the illusion of depth. One technique called **linear perspective** directs attention to a vanishing point, the spot at which parallel lines receding from the eye of the observer seem to come together (see fig. 34). In another technique called **aerial** or **atmospheric perspective**, closer objects are shown in greater detail and in sharper focus than distant ones (see fig. 35). Sometimes objects and figures are placed in overlapping planes so that the closer ones partially block the distant ones from view. All these techniques reinforce the sense of three dimensions.

Like skilled painters, filmmakers use principles of classical composition to guide the viewer's eye to the important areas of the work. Usually the human eye is attracted to the center of any marked-out space (see fig. 36). But if the filmmaker places a prominent figure at the top of the frame, or adds a distinct color such as red to the lower left portion of the picture, or puts a brightly lit object in the upper right part of the image, then the viewer's attention will be pulled to that area. In a black-and-white film, the eye will be attracted to lighter areas in the frame, although the center of the frame continues to be important and is usually reserved for the most significant information. In the absence of other indicators, people in European-influenced cultures, in which words are read from left to right, read pictures along the same directional lines (see fig. 37). That eye movement gives priority to design elements located on the left of the frame over those on the right. All these elements—dominance of the center, color, lit areas, priority of left over right and of the top over the bottom of the frame—draw the viewer's attention to information emotionally or dramatically significant. No matter what graphic details might be used to attract attention in a film, a moving subject is always dominant, drawing the spectator's eye to the action.

■ Composition in Depth

The composition of a single shot depends on the design of the *mise en scène* and technical decisions (choice of lens, camera angle, and camera distance) made by the director and cinematographer to capture that design on film. This involves more than just the horizontal and vertical dimensions of the screen. Depth must be taken into consideration, as filmmakers always compose the frame with this third "illusory" dimension in mind.

Figure 36. My Darling Clementine (d. John Ford, 1946). Because Wyatt Earp (Henry Fonda) is in the center of the shot, his head framed by the mirror behind him, the spectator's eye is drawn to him.

The camera records action that has been arranged and takes place in three dimensions, and then the filmed material is projected onto a two-dimensional screen. Because the actual filming records real space, the camera automatically captures a certain amount of three-dimensionality. When certain constructed sets are used, however, the illusion is often incomplete. In such cases, the physical arrangement of people and objects will enhance or diminish the effect of realistic, three-dimensional space. Principles of perspective enhance three-dimensionality: overlapping planes, layering and backlighting subjects, arranging subjects along lines to a vanishing point, and lighting the background. These techniques are especially noticeable in films using sets with painted backdrops, rear screen projection, or miniatures.

As pointed out in Chapter 2, the selected camera lens affects the depth of the image. The telephoto lens flattens out the natural depth of a set or location, while the wide-angle lens intensifies it. This is especially true in a locale where actors and objects can be arranged in three planes: foreground, middleground and background. When the image is projected onto a wide, slightly curved screen, the maximum impact of artificial perspective is achieved, and the shot looks three-dimensional.

Figure 37. Rear Window (d. Alfred Hitchcock, 1957). The shot is designed to draw the viewer's eye from James Stewart in the dominant area at left foreground to the center of the image, where his open window frames the windows belonging to his neighbors across the courtyard.

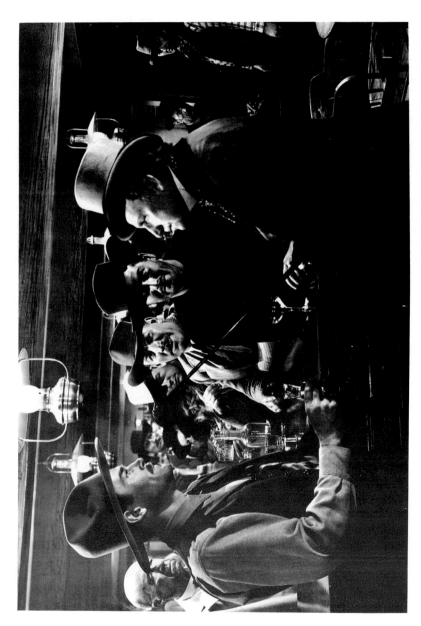

Figure 38. My Darling Clementine. Despite the "weight" provided by the line of men at the bar in this deep focus shot, the exact center of the frame is between Victor Mature and Ward Bond, whose eyeline gazes are exactly opposed. The walking stick, overhead lanterns, and light on the rear wall shift the balance of the frame to Wyatt Earp (Henry Fonda).

To "edit in depth" refers to designing and shooting a scene in a continuous take while the action moves through the three visual planes; the director has no intention of fragmenting or cutting the scene later in the editing room. This sets up a certain realism by approximating the way that people look at unfolding events—more like "life in a long take" rather than in pieces. The uncut, long sequences that employ *mise en scène* as the basis of organization allow relationships to form through the use of deep-focus photography. For example, in *Citizen Kane*, Orson Welles uses composition in depth in the well-known scene in which Mrs. Kane signs Charles away to the banker Thatcher. Charles, playing in the snow, is framed by the window of the boarding house. He is in the background, in focus, at the center of the frame. While he plays, carefree, his future and his fate are being decided by his father, in focus, in the middleground and his mother and Thatcher in the foreground, also in focus. In this way, the connection among them is made in a single shot through deep-focus photography.

Even in movies that are supposedly strictly realistic, filmmakers often deliberately manipulate information, minimizing background and depth to concentrate on details. Backgrounds may be eliminated by use of a close-up or may be shot out of focus. In a rack or pulled focus shot, the sharply focused image in one plane gradually blurs as focus is "pulled" to bring detail in another plane into focus—a face in the crowd, a gun in an assassin's hand, a letter in a jilted lover's hand. But in most feature films, the realistic-looking space created by artificial perspective serves as a foundation and holds the imaginary world of the story together (see fig. 38).

■ Screen Size

When composing a shot, the director must consider **screen size** because the screen, like a picture frame, sets the limits of the field of vision and affects the shape of the image. Composition must be modified to take advantage of the proportions of the screen. For the first fifty years of production, the screen was a standard rectangle with an **aspect ratio**, the ratio of the width to the height of the image, of 1.33:1 (one and a third times wider than its height). Because the Academy of Motion Picture Arts and Sciences favored this screen shape, it was called the **Academy aperture**. Academy members thought this screen size and shape offered nearly perfect proportions for well-balanced composition. Most Hollywood productions before 1950 were composed according to the Academy ratio.

In the 1950s, television came along and it, too, began using this ratio sometimes referred to as the Golden Mean. But when television programming began to cut into the audience share of the movies, film producers decided to distinguish their product from the intruder's shows. One tactic was to play up the difference between the "big screen" and the "little box." Motion picture production moved into extremes of big screen production. To make the best use of the wide screen, the industry developed formats such as Cinerama and Todd-AO, which were more than twice as wide as they were high.

Initially widescreen formats were reserved for big-budget, spectacular extravaganzas, but as the film industry adjusted to the permanent presence of television, the wider screen became the standard format for almost all feature production. The changes in screen size affected both production and composition. First of all, great screen width increases the impression of depth and lends itself to the use of deep focus and composition in depth. Second, montage editing and the master-shot sequence, with its close-up inserts, do not work well on the wide screen. Cinematographers have problems composing close-ups and two-shots for the large, horizontal-shaped space — a format best suited for filming rattlesnakes, director John Ford quipped. Editors discovered that quick cutting confused viewers, who could not absorb the increased amount of visual information unless the pace was slower. Third, a larger image size lends itself to spacious locations and elaborate *mise en scène* in comparison to the more confined frames of the Academy ratio and television screen.

Today producers are making films with television, video, laserdisc, and DVD distribution in mind. Because American viewers prefer images filling their entire television screen, they tend to favor pan-and-scan or cropped film-to-video transfers instead of letterboxed ones. Yet only letterboxing preserves the original aspect ratio of widescreen films and leaves their compositions intact. Instead of taking advantage of the large canvas offered by these formats, cautious directors resort to **centralized composition**, confining the characters and action to the middle of the frame. Camera lenses are imprinted with marks showing the cinematographer exactly what part of the composition will remain in the television frame after the film images are transferred, thus ensuring minimal loss of information.

■ Graphic Elements

Aware of classical composition and principles of graphic design in art, filmmakers incorporate these concepts when designing the film image. Directors recognize—at times intuitively, at times consciously—the ways in which composition affects the meaning of the shot. Sergei Eisenstein acknowledged that **symmetrical compositions**—centered, static, circular or parallel forms—convey a sense of balance, harmony, and stability (see fig. 39). **Asymmetrical compositions** consist of off-center elements,

Figure 39. 2001: A Space Odyssey. A set using perfect symmetry for a balanced composition.

Figure 40. *The Battleship Potemkin.* Eisenstein preferred the dynamism of asymmetrical composition, because it conveyed his view of a world in chaos and underlined his commitment to radical filmmaking. In the Odessa Steps sequence, a child lying wounded on the steps extends out of frame, disturbing the balance of the shot.

unbalanced arrangements of objects, and diagonals (see fig. 40) — generating tension, anxiety, and excitement.

Shapes and forms, which are aesthetically pleasing to a viewer's eye, often carry secondary meanings. **Circles** are a traditional literary and visual form and, when used either as a graphic element or in the movement of the camera, might establish the cyclical nature of a situation or convey a sense of unity. **Triangular compositions** often delineate relationships among three or more people, with the most significant person placed at the apex of the triangle (see fig. 41). The shadow of Venetian blinds on a wall resembles prison bars and is often used in thrillers to symbolize or foreshadow entrapment. Darkness and light in a shot may dissect a person's face or the decor and suggest the opposition between good and evil. Distortions of space and disordered framing may symbolize dislocation or anxiety.

A shot in which activity and objects spill over the edges of the frame works to reinforce the realism of a scene. Such a shot suggests more going on than the camera can capture and that the events are not staged. The objects and characters are not arranged in neatly balanced places in

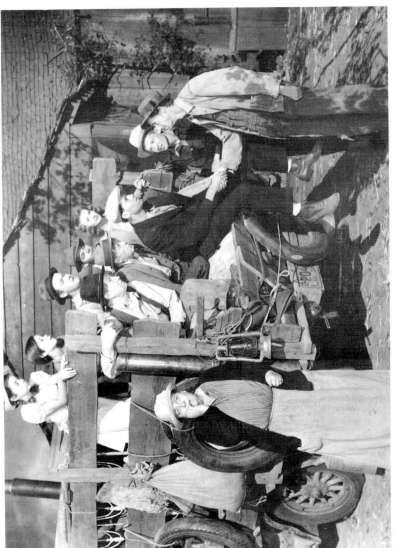

Figure 41. *The Grapes of Wrath* (d. John Ford, 1940). John Ford preferred symmetrical compositions depicting a world of order, tradition, and stability. One side of this triangular composition is formed by the strong diagonal line of the Joad family on the back of the truck, their gazes converging on Casey (John Carradine) at the apex. Tom Joad (Henry Fonda) shakes hands with him, while Ma Joad (Jane Darwell), on the left, completes the triangle. The triangular framing suggests a balance between anxiety and hope.

Figure 42. The Killing Fields (d. Roland Joffe, 1984). The "uncomposed" or loose composition shows the spill of action beyond the limits of the frame. This open form adds realism to the scene. While action occurs in the foreground, middleground, and background, the bars (out of focus) in the extreme foreground form a barrier, trapping the running figures. Figuratively, the audience is separated from the fleeing group. Dith Pran, the main character, is neatly outlined in the center of the frame, but in the film, the scene is one of movement and near chaos.

© 1984 Goldcrest Films and Television Limited

the frame, but instead appear to be organized randomly in what is called an open form (see fig. 42). In *The Battle of Algiers* (1966), Gillo Pontecorvo used this kind of uncomposed or loose composition in his filming to convey the hectic, unplanned quality of a situation, as though there were no time to compose, because "life was going by too fast." Steven Soderbergh took the same approach when shooting *Traffic*, hoping the audience would experience the film as though events were happening right in front of them. Shooting with two handheld cameras and available light, Soderbergh served as his own D.P., working quickly using the "run-and-gun" approach. His loose compositions give the drama a directness and immediacy that enhance the realism of the drug war on screen.

■ Dynamic Composition

The filmmaker composes space so that it seems real and continuous by using **deep-focus photography**, which keeps images in all planes in

Figure 43. *Touch of Evil* (d. Orson Welles, 1958). The shadows of the Venetian blinds on the wall and the strong key light on Vargas's (Charlton Heston) face are typical of *film noir* lighting. Detective Hank Quinlan's (Orson Welles) hat masks his eyes, suggesting his deceit, which is borne out in the course of the car bomb investigation. Here, at a turning point in the film, narcotics agent Vargas discovers Quinlan planting a stick of dynamite as false evidence.

sharp focus and maximizes perspective, and by editing shots together to create a sense of unified place. Because film depends upon movement, the composition of the image cannot be described on the basis of just one "frozen" picture. Shots must be looked at in terms of dynamic composition, the changing relationship among a number of graphic elements in motion. The spectator's natural tendency to notice motion governs the dominant point of interest within the frame, and so motion will inevitably change the balance of the frame composition.

The opening shot of Orson Welles's *Touch of Evil* (1958) provides a vivid example of dynamic composition used in place of conventional editing. Within a single take, Welles incorporates his signature dramatic close-ups, strong angles, and low-key lighting (see fig. 43). Accompanied by a musical and rhythmic soundtrack, the tracking shot reveals a man planting a bomb in the trunk of a car and then links two couples—one pair now driving in the car and the other walking on the street—whose paths converge as they arrive simultaneously at a border crossing. In this uncut shot, Welles relies on flowing camera movement instead of editing to create curiosity and establish suspense. His use of dynamic composition enhances the connection between the two couples, linking them spatially and causally, as they move toward an inevitable intersection of their lives and death. In this three-minute sequence, the choreography of the moving camera shapes and intensifies the action, and forces the viewer to notice changing parts of the frame.

Making a film is a complex undertaking. Locations and convincing sets, under the supervision of a production designer, must meet the director's specifications and must accommodate the camera and actors. Lighting literally and figuratively illuminates the scene and often adds a separate level of meaning through its design. The actors must perform and maintain their roles from one take to the next. Everything that occurs in front of the camera — the *mise en scène* — must be carefully planned. All significant information, from concrete details to the most subtle levels of thematic suggestion, must be captured in the images on the screen.

Chapter 5

Editing

When film theorists compare filmmaking to writing, they make the analogy that the camera is similar to a pen and editing establishes a specific "grammar." Arranging shots into sequences is like putting words together into sentences, and, as in writing, control of the arrangement helps the author express a personal vision. Anyone who has experience with a word processing program knows how easily material can be rearranged and how each arrangement affects the meaning of what is written. In many ways film editing is similar, even insofar as today's professional editors use highly sophisticated computerized editing systems.

To tell a story with clarity and impact, the filmmaker, like the writer, must decide what material to use and in what order. By juxtaposing pieces of film—putting them next to each other in a specific order—**editing** organizes single shots into sequences and sequences into a coherent work. Just as writers edit by cutting and pasting words, sentences, and paragraphs, so do film editors trim, move, and reorganize footage. This process is not limited to assembling and reassembling bits of information. Editing develops rhythm and pace, unity of space and time, and visual and aural relationships. And just as writing is governed by principles of syntax, film editing has standards and conventions.

When the cinema began in 1895, the first filmmakers did not edit. They would set the camera up far enough away from the action to get it all into the frame and shoot until the roll of film ran out. As a result, the camera was like the spectator in a theater, seated in the orchestra center, viewing the whole stage—with characters entering and leaving the scene — from that one vantage point. Short skits, gags, and playlets that could be staged over a short time were recorded and then projected. In fact the movies originally borrowed their ideas and terminology from the theater: *scene, set, decor, producer,* and *director* entered the vocabulary of film.

By 1902 several pioneer film directors had begun to string shots together, creating scenes that were long enough to develop action into a story. They recognized the medium's potential for showing events that took place in more than one location at the same time. Through parallel editing, spectators could see action filmed at several different sites but they were still stuck in Row M Center watching the performance in long shot. About ten years later, D.W. Griffith began to explore the expressive power of the close-up and the medium shot, interrupting the action from time to time to cut in to a close-up of a character's emotion-filled face. "Cutting in" and "cutting away" from shots quickly became standard procedure in narrative filmmaking.

These filmmakers established the **shot** as the basic unit of film construction. They took a single shot and connected it to others, most often through a straight cut, to form sequences that were internally coherent and unified by action, location, or character. Their films told stories and conveyed factual information through complex relationships between sequences.

■ The Kuleshov Effect: An Experiment in Editing

Just after the 1917 Russian Revolution, Soviet filmmakers began to consider and experiment with the power of film. The use of the close-up, introduced by Griffith, inspired an experiment in editing that Soviet director Lev Kuleshov supposedly conducted in the 1920s. As the French film historian Jean Mitry tells in his book, *Esthétique et psychologie du cinéma*, Kuleshov purposely selected a close-up shot of an actor with a vague look on his face and made three copies of it. He spliced the first copy to a shot of a plate of soup (and here is where versions of the story vary), the second copy to a shot of a man's corpse lying face down on the ground, and the third to a shot of a half-nude woman posed lasciviously on a couch. He then spliced all the shots together so that the image of the actor's face appeared between each of the other shots. According to observers' reports (and there is no other documentation), everyone who saw the sequence read it as that of a brilliant actor expressing his deepest feelings, first of desperate hunger, then of pity, and then of desire. The sequence was read in this way even though the look on the actor's face was exactly the same, since exactly the same shot was cut in each time. Whether the story is true or not, the psychology of perception supports the notion that viewers' own feelings and understanding determine their interpretation of material in a sequence. Kuleshov himself reasoned that a shot acquires a value beyond its photographed reality when juxtaposed to other shots. Editing produces new meanings and can "create" an actor's performance. This became known as the Kuleshov effect.

Alfred Hitchcock recreated the Kuleshov effect in *Rear Window* (1954). Confined to a wheelchair because of a broken leg, L.B. Jeffries (James Stewart) passes his time looking out his apartment window at his neighbors through binoculars and a telephoto camera lens. He sees a musician working, newlyweds moving into an apartment, a woman drinking alone, a dancer practicing ballet, a couple bickering. Hitchcock cuts back and forth from shots of each person's activities to Jeff's face (see fig. 44). As in the original experiment, the shot of Jeff's face is the same one repeated several times. Hitchcock intended the audience to read the range of Jeff's emotions: pity, approval, amusement, curiosity. In fact the actor's look does seem to change depending on which scene he is looking at. As Kuleshov's experiment was meant to prove, the viewer's identification with the hero and response to the emotional content of the scene depends on the sequence of shots.

■ Soviet Montage

A student of Kuleshov, Sergei Eisenstein studied the work of D.W. Griffith. He considered the theoretical issues underlying Griffith's practice and realized that editing was the most significant element in cinema, the one that distinguishes it from other forms like painting, literature, and theater. Eisenstein proposed that the film medium allows individual shots to be assembled and then perceived simultaneously by the spectator. He compared editing to the Japanese ideogram, in which the hieroglyph of water placed next to the hieroglyph, or picture, of an eye signifies "to weep." The combination is not the sum of the two images but a new idea resulting from their fusion.

Instead of assembling shots to create seamless realism, Eisenstein put them together so they would "collide" with one another, and thereby gain new meaning. His theory of **montage** (the term comes from the French *monter*, to mount or assemble, as in to mount a picture or to assemble a machine) operated according to the Marxist dialectic of history: two colliding forces, thesis and antithesis, produce a new phenomenon, or synthesis, greater than and different from their individual parts. As described in *Film Form*, Eisenstein's collection of twelve essays on the aesthetics of filmmaking written between 1928 and 1945, his collision-

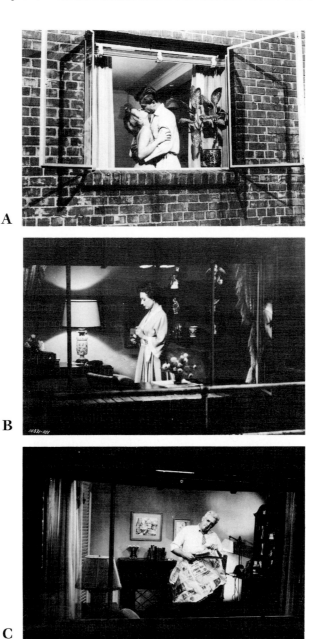

Figure 44 A-C. Rear Window. Hitchcock's version of the
Kuleshov effect intercuts the same shot of James
Stewart's face (fig. 44 D), as he looks through the
telephoto lens of his camera, with shots of various
activities in the apartments across the courtyard.

Figure 44 D. Rear Window. Jeff (James Stewart) seems to respond differently to each of the scenes.

and-contrast methodology implements many types of visual counterpoint including graphic, spatial, light, and tempo conflict, and conflict of planes and volumes (see fig. 45). Since Eisenstein's montage is distinguished by the use of many short takes edited together in sequences of rapidly changing images, his work is the basis of the editing style used in today's music videos.

■ The Odessa Steps Sequence

The Odessa Steps sequence from Eisenstein's film *The Battleship Potemkin* (1925) illustrates this "montage of conflict," as his theory became known. The soldiers of the Czar march down the central steps in the city of Odessa and move against its population to break up a minor demonstration. The sequence intends to represent the terror of the people and the faceless brutality of the czarist regime. Eisenstein expands time by overlapping the action and inserting details—faces, rifles, falling bodies —to suggest the psychological state and response of the victims.

Each shot has an **internal rhythm** determined by camera movement and/or the action within the frame. Eisenstein incorporated internal rhythm in the composition of his shots. Then, during the editing process, he juxtaposed the shots to mark out every possible contrast: between light and dark forms, between rounded and angular shapes, between the rhythmic downward march of the soldiers and the chaotic flight of the populace, between high and low angle and close and distant shots. The tension and conflict between the people and the Czar's soldiers are thereby presented and reinforced—all without dialogue, entirely through editing.

External rhythm develops from the duration of each shot. The fast-paced sequence on the Odessa Steps fragments action by joining shots of short running time, and thereby creates tension. The editing breaks down the action into component parts. Photographed from a slight low angle, the soldiers move in formation down a long flight of steps. The sequence cuts to a shot of their rifles with bayonets fixed. Several diagonals—the downward movement of the soldiers, the steps, the rifles—are in opposition to each other. Eisenstein cuts to a woman whose child has been shot. She lifts up the wounded child and marches back up the stairs, her movement and direction opposing and contrasting to that of the soldiers. A momentary hesitation in the downward movement ends when the soldiers fire on the crowd.

The climax of the sequence comes with a cut to a woman shot while trying to move her baby out of harm's way. A series of close-ups follow, using matches as well as contrasts between graphic shapes: on the face of the mother, on the baby in the carriage, on the mass of people, on the boots of the soldiers, on the wheels of the baby carriage, back on the face

*Figure 45. **The Battleship Potemkin.** In the Odessa Steps sequence, Eisenstein creates a montage of conflict by contrasting different graphic patterns, camera angles and distances, and volumes. The circular shape of the mother's head and mouth (B and D) is repeated in the wheels of the baby carriage (C) and the belt clasp (F). These conflict with the diagonal pattern formed by the soldiers and the angle of the perpendicular rifles (A). Shots C and E combine contrasting patterns: the round carriage wheel is on the edge of the diagonal step (C); townspeople and Cossacks swirl against the strong horizontal lines of the steps (E). Shots B and C, C and D, and D and E juxtapose low angle and high angle shots. D and E also establish conflicts of volume, camera distance, and tempo: the close-up of the mother slowly moving her head counterpoints the extreme long shot of the fleeing crowd. The montage establishes the opposition between the soldiers and the townspeople through graphic design, camerawork, and editing.*

of the mother and then on her hands, clutching her belt where she has been hit, finally on the circular wheels of the carriage (see fig. 45). The carriage teeters on the steps, its wheels contrasting with the diagonal of the step. The mother falls; all resistance by the population collapses.

At that point, the baby carriage, with no one to hold it, careens dramatically down the steps. The shots now cut from the carriage descending the steps, to the baby in the carriage, to a close-up on the carriage wheels, to the faces of horrified citizens, but always returning to the soldiers moving relentlessly down the steps. The sequence ends with the well-known close-up of the Cossack raising his sword against an old woman whose broken pince-nez eye glasses and bloodied eye imply his action and testify to its violence, although the blow itself is not shown on the screen. The viewer's imagination and emotions fill in the unseen material.

■ Hollywood Montage

The Odessa Steps sequence is the most analyzed, discussed, and familiar piece of film in cinema history. The sequence is so well known that later directors alluded to it in their own films. Woody Allen makes a brief, humorous reference to it in *Bananas* (1971). In *The Untouchables* (1987), Brian De Palma reworks the sequence in 1930s gangster style. These are tributes to Eisenstein by filmmakers who studied the history of cinema.

For the American industry, the term **Hollywood montage** means any sequence of rapidly edited images suggesting the passage of time or a series of events. It sketches but does not develop information about characters. In *Casablanca* a flashback montage presents Rick's memory of his romance with Ilsa: dissolves link the shots of the couple driving in Paris, walking along the river Seine, and dancing in a nightclub. The montage lends a dreamlike quality to the memory and suggests the timelessness of the lovers' relationship. In contrast to that romantic mood, Alfred Hitchcock used the Soviet filmmakers' techniques to produce suspense, tension, and horror: the series of rapid cuts in the shower sequence in *Psycho* is a good example.

■ Classical Editing

The Hollywood film industry grew up as a storytelling medium, something like the popular novel. Contrary to the Soviet experiments, Hollywood used principles of **continuity editing** to make the story flow smoothly, so the action would move along without obvious or jarring interruptions. This approach encourages viewers to identify with the central characters and draws them into the narrative. As a result, viewers receive the film material in a passive state that allows only emotional reaction and stifles critical thinking. Hollywood movies avoided calling attention to the act of filming, and carefully constructed the forward movement of the story through specific techniques that ensured continuity and narrative progression. American filmmakers thought viewers had to be cued to changes in place, time, and point of view but always without breaking narrative continuity, the smooth forward movement of story or event.

The **continuity** or **script supervisor** ensures visual consistency as the action progresses from shot to shot, making sure, for example, that the characters are dressed exactly the same way in a scene. Since scenes are often filmed hours or days or weeks apart, the supervisor must watch over and record everything captured by the camera in order to avoid mismatches from one take to the next. Due to continuity errors, the length of Judy Garland's hair changes in the same scene of *The Wizard of Oz*: Dorothy's braids are mid-length when she is brought to the Wicked Witch's castle, down to her waist when Toto runs away, and at shoulder length when the witch later turns over the hourglass. However, incongruous or anachronistic discrepancies may be intentionally included for humor, emphasis, or as an experiment. In *Moulin Rouge* (2001), a postmodern musical, Baz Luhrmann inserted contemporary elements like modern popular songs and self-conscious references into the 19th-century Paris setting.

Fairly strict rules govern the film techniques ensuring continuity and narrative progression. In the case of continuity, the goal is to make editing invisible in order to enhance narrative continuity. The conventions of continuity editing include sequences based on the match cut, the shot/reverse shot, and the master shot. In the case of narrative progression, the goal is to advance the story and assure suspense and identification. Sequential action, crosscutting, flashbacks and flash forwards serve narrative functions of moving the story forward. Classical editing guides the viewer through the story by emphasizing what is emotionally and dramatically significant.

■ The Match Cut

The basic way to achieve smooth editing is through the **match cut**, the foundation of all continuity cutting. The editor joins two shots that match according to the direction of the camera movement, action, direction of the glance, or by similar graphic elements. Usually these matches are based on screen direction: a character, object, or the camera in one shot moves in the same direction in the next. A rider on a horse or in a car, moving from screen right to screen left, will be picked up in the next shot, continuing from right to left. If the camera rather than the character is moving—perhaps panning from right to left—the movement will continue in the next shot from right to left. A shot of a ball rolling from screen right to left may be cut to a shot of a wheel rolling in the same direction. When the object is stationary, the cut, based on shape alone, is called a **form cut.**

In *Dances With Wolves* (1990), the opening sequence set during the Civil War offers many shots of chaotic circumstances. Despite the confusion, at certain points the camera movement is in the same direction from cut to cut and unifies the action. Lieutenant John Dunbar (Kevin Costner) later joins a supply wagon headed for the farthest military outpost on the western frontier. A series of shots shows the wagon moving from screen left to screen right. Then, in one shot, it gradually turns and, in successive shots, begins to travel from screen right to screen left. In this case, the direction of the wagon's movement across the screen, matched from shot to shot, indicates the westward journey deep into the wilderness that ends in Dunbar's remaining alone at the abandoned fort.

Match on action requires that the cut be made at a precise moment: as the first shot ends, the action continues in the second shot which, incidentally, must be filmed from a different distance or angle. Cuts are not made out of the blue, just anywhere in the scene. Normally they are made during a motion or a gesture, while a character sits down or stands up, enters or exits a scene. Again in *Dances With Wolves*, on the first morning at the abandoned outpost, Lieutenant Dunbar goes to get some water. Picking up a bucket, he slowly makes his way to a pond. A long shot shows him as he kneels at the pond's edge, grabs the side of the bucket, and begins to lift it towards the water. Cut to a medium shot of him as he continues the action of placing the bucket in the water; the match on action makes the edit invisible. Suddenly, as something catches his attention, Dunbar freezes and slowly turns his head to the left, as the camera pulls back and reveals deer horns sticking up through the water. The next cut, an eyeline match, reveals the head of the dead animal suspended just beneath the surface. Startled for the second time that morning, and upset by indications of the death and destruction of the fort's inhabitants, Dunbar jumps back, drops the bucket, and staggers from the pond.

The eyeline match requires a cut based on the line and direction of the glance rather than on the direction of movement. It requires a **point-of-view (POV) shot**, also called a **subjective shot** or **first-person shot**. The shot may be taken from any distance or angle as long as it logically represents what the character is supposed to be seeing, his or her subjective point of view. In the first shot, a person looks off-screen. The second shot depicts an image of a location, person, or object. The viewer reads the second image as what the person is looking at because of the eyeline match. Sometimes a cut moves back to the face of the character.

An illustration of the classic use of the eyeline match cut appears in a sequence of *Casablanca*. Rick (Humphrey Bogart), hearing the song "As Time Goes By," angrily walks over to the piano and starts to tell Sam (Dooley Wilson) to stop playing. Sam gestures with his head toward the right. Rick, picking up on the gesture, looks in the same direction, and his eyes meet . . . (cut) . . . Ilsa's (Ingrid Bergman), whose gaze, in a reverse-angle shot, meets his. Toward the end of the film, another sequence shows both the bonds and the tensions among Rick, Ilsa, and Ilsa's husband, Victor Laszlo (Paul Henreid). The sequence begins at the airport with a medium shot of the three standing on the runway (see fig. 27). Cut to a plane revving its motor. As the sound of the plane becomes noticeable, the sequence cuts to a close-up of Rick as he looks to the right and then turns his head slightly from left to right. This is followed by a quick dissolve to Ilsa, who, in a matching close-up, is also looking to her right toward the plane. She turns almost 180 degrees until her glance lines up with Rick's. A cut to a close-up of Rick, meeting her glance, establishes their emotional connection. Then Rick's gaze shifts. He turns back slightly, raises his eyes, and looks off-screen. Cut to a close-up of Ilsa who closes her eyes for a moment and then opens them, seeming to return his glance. A quick dissolve to a slightly more distant close-up of Victor shows that he is the point on which both Rick and Ilsa's glances converge. Victor looks only at Ilsa. The final shot of the sequence shows all three of them looking at one another. This exchange of glances recapitulates the whole story — the love triangle, the progression of the relationships, the outcome of the story.

In certain cases the framing and composition of the POV shot also convey the character's mood, perspective, and physical or psychological state. A point-of-view sequence indicates, for example, Alicia's sickness from arsenic poisoning in *Notorious*, the aging doorman's hangover in *The Last Laugh* (see fig. 46), and Scottie Ferguson's pathological fear of heights in *Vertigo*. The shot offers a point of view through the spectator's alignment with the camera's position. Through the eyeline match, the viewer's position changes from the first shot where she or he observes the character to the second where she or he sees what the character is seeing and, therefore, is forced to identify with the character.

Matching graphic elements as the basis for a cut depends on a design factor—a circle, a square, a diagonal form or pattern—repeated from one shot to another. In Stanley Kubrick's *2001: A Space Odyssey* (1968), the prehistoric man flings a bone, which he has just used on another creature, high into the air. The bone spins and turns in slow motion, end over end. At this point, Kubrick cuts to a spacecraft of the same shape in the same place in the frame. Four million years have passed in an instant, and another tool of man floats through the skies. Another film that extensively uses form cuts and matching graphic elements for transition and symbolic overtones is Jean-Jacques Annaud's *The Bear* (1988).

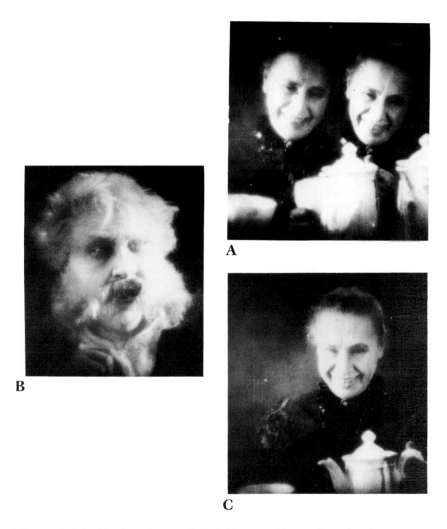

Figure 46 A-C. The Last Laugh (d. F.W. Murnau, 1924). The aging doorman's (Emil Jannings) neighbor offers him coffee. Shot A shows her through his eyes, the double image conveying the subjective experience of his hangover. He rubs his eyes, looks again (B), and then his vision returns to normal (C).

■ The Shot/Reverse Shot

The **shot/reverse shot** cuts together two or more shots of a conversation. The first shot records the speaker, who faces the camera, talking to another person whose back may be included in the shot. The reverse shot is taken from the angle opposite or nearly opposite to it. Sometimes the framing is over one character's shoulder and composed so that the spectator is, in effect, listening in on the conversation. Sometimes the point of view alternates between the characters, and the two points of view are matched through eyeline direction.

■ The Master-Shot Sequence

A **master shot** records an entire scene in one take without interruption. For many years this was an accepted procedure in Hollywood. Closer shots are later edited into the master to produce a complete sequence, a **master-shot sequence**. The standard arrangement of shots begins with a long shot, called an **establishing shot** because it establishes the context—the dramatic situation and the location—and orients the viewer. Then the editor cuts to a medium shot of the same subject, followed by a cut to a close shot of the same subject or by shots from other angles and distances. The editor returns to the establishing shot whenever necessary to remind the viewer of the context.

In the 1930s and 1940s, even when this type of editing was common, directors preferred to vary the angle and distance of subsequent shots for dramatic purposes. Today's filmmaking practice is much more flexible and tends to break this predictable sequence of shots. Some filmmakers withhold the establishing shot until later in the sequence. Those working in the experimental cinema or committed to applying film theory to their practice deliberately set out to destroy audience expectations. They call into question the place of the filmmaker and the spectator by refusing to use the master sequence, creating new connections and forcing the viewer to think about the editing.

■ Transitional Devices

Transitional devices cue the viewer to changes in time, place, and action, from shot to shot and sequence to sequence. They function on the same principles of continuity as do other techniques of classical editing: namely, to ensure the smooth forward flow of the narrative. Transitional devices move the viewer from one sequence to the next sequence and, although not precisely invisible, they were established as transitions by convention. Among the most common of these devices are the fade, dissolve, and wipe.

The **fade-out** or fade to black, in which the image darkens to black, provides a gentle shift between shots. This device resembles the quiet fall of a theater curtain between acts of a play, and, in film, marks the end of a segment of action. The **fade-in**, in which the blackness lightens

into an image of a new scene in a new location, almost always follows—
like a theater curtain going up on the next act.

The **dissolve** connects rather than separates because two images—of
locations, character, or action—are superimposed on one another and
appear together on the screen for some period of time. One of the most
famous transitions in cinema occurs in *Psycho*: Hitchcock ends the shower
sequence with a quick dissolve from a close-up on the circle of the shower
drain to a close-up on the circular shape of the murdered woman's open
eye, before the camera slowly pulls back to reveal her whole face. At the
end of the film, in another famous but barely perceptible connection, the
face of Norman Bates's mummified mother is subtly superimposed over
his face. The dissolve visually reinforces the special bond between them.
This superimposed image connects to yet another narrative element, as
the faces of Norman and "mother" dissolve into the film's final shot: the
murdered woman's car being dredged from the swamp.

The dissolve to begin a flashback sequence or to associate two images,
and the fade to show the passage of time or a change of location, were
like punctuation marks in writing and just as commonplace. They were
developed and applied fairly consistently until the 1960s. But by then,
films began to use transitional devices less frequently, perhaps because
more than a decade of constant exposure to relatively innovative TV advertising had increased the sophistication of viewers who could now read
complex image sequences.

Other transitional devices were used less often and only in specific
contexts, usually as a visual turn in musicals and comedies. The **iris**, a
dark circular matte either widening into an image or narrowing to isolate a detail in the larger picture, was one of the earliest cinematic devices
and already out of fashion by the 1930s. The **wipe** consists of one image
moving across the screen and "wiping off" the one already there. In the
flip frame, the image reverses or flips over to reveal another. These are
rarely used today.

When these transitional devices are used in contemporary films, they
are conspicuous and break the illusion of reality by calling attention to
the filmmaking process. The rerelease of *The Manchurian Candidate*, a
film made in 1962 but out of circulation for about twenty-five years, revealed how much shooting and editing styles had changed over the
intervening time. The devices are used expressively: dissolves introduce
the characters' nightmares as well as changes in location and time, and
dramatic camera angles are juxtaposed to impart emotional intensity to
sequences. One sequence, edited as a series of rapid cuts followed by two
quick wipes, shows Raymond Shaw's (Laurence Harvey) long, deliberate
climb to the top of Madison Square Garden. To the modern viewer these
devices may seem intrusive and unrealistic, but this stylized editing provides dramatic and emotional intensity.

Until recently, the **jump cut** was only used in experimental filmmaking. In an industry that operated according to the principles of invisible editing, the jump-cut was an obvious error to be avoided. It was usually seen only when the film broke down during a screening and lost a few frames so that movement seemed to "jump" forward in the repaired footage. In 1959 Jean-Luc Godard changed all that in his seminal film *Breathless* by deliberately using the jump-cut as a break with the conventions of classical editing. Mismatches in action and changes in angle make the film jump slightly from one shot to the next, giving the action an irregular quality that tends to undermine the film's gangster story, sometimes in a humorous way. Godard calls attention to the act of cutting, and thereby challenges notions of invisible editing that had dominated filmmaking until then. He later defended his decision by comparing the disorientation of film audiences to the emotional detachment of theater audiences at performances of Bertoldt Brecht's works: spectator **distanciation** encourages a more thoughtful response to the material. The acceptance of *Breathless* by a wide audience, Godard's increasing influence and prestige as a theoretician and experimental narrative filmmaker, and the recognition of alternative cinema by the art community and universities brought the jump-cut and other anti-classical cinematic devices into the commercial cinema and television—especially in the form of music videos.

■ Narrative Progression

One of the main functions of editing is to advance the narrative. Any type of film can be narrative, that is, can tell a story. The story may be imaginary, in which case it is fiction, or it may document real events, in which case it is nonfiction. Any thread of information that links events together by time-sequence is narrative. The sentence "the Queen died, and the King died" is a naming of events. The sentence "the Queen died, and *then* the King died" is a chronological linking of events. The sentence "the Queen died, and *then* the King died *of grief*" implies causality. Newspaper stories, television news reports, and some advertisements are almost always presented as narratives—using dramatic elements and stating or implying sequence and cause. In fact, news reports use an approach like that of television soap operas to present events, even events as serious as the terrorist attacks that destroyed the World Trade Center and part of the Pentagon. They create suspense so the audience will "tune in to find out what happens next."

The **straight cut** is the most basic way to advance the story, as action progresses in a chronological time frame. In *Beverly Hills Cop* (1984), for example, the opening establishes Detroit as the location. Planning to investigate the murder of his pal, Axel Foley (Eddie Murphy) tells his boss that he wants to take the vacation time coming to him. His boss agrees but warns: "If you butt into this case, it'll be the longest vacation you ever heard of." The camera holds for a moment on Foley while a musical beat comes up on the soundtrack and then, in a straight cut, the location changes from the Detroit street at night to a low angle shot of stately royal palm trees against a brilliant blue sky, an image that defines Beverly Hills.

Crosscutting or **parallel editing** also furthers narrative. The technique connects action taking place at several different locations and suggests simultaneity, that the actions are taking place at the same time and will converge. This produces suspense. In the early days of cinema, cliffhangers—movie serials like *The Perils of Pauline*—offered weekly variations on this typical crosscut sequence: a shot of the heroine tied to the railroad tracks; cut to a shot of the train coming toward her; another cut to the hero riding to her rescue. The actions did converge, of course, usually for a successful outcome. D. W. Griffith's *The Lonedale Operator* (1908) crosscuts among four locations to show suspenseful action taking place all at the same time: the telegraph office at the Lonedale train station where a young woman is working, an area outside the station where the robbers are lurking in an attempt to break into the office, another telegraph office farther down the train line where another operator receives the telegraphed call for help from the Lonedale operator, and the train on which a young engineer races to her rescue.

Alfred Hitchcock always relied on crosscutting to generate suspense and advance the story. In one sequence in *Notorious*, Alicia (Ingrid Bergman) and Devlin (Cary Grant) are searching the wine cellar. The shots alternate between the couple in the cellar looking for evidence of foul play and the party above where the champagne is beginning to run low. Because the host may need to get more wine, Alicia, keeping watch for Devlin, expresses the anxiety, also building in the viewer, over the possible arrival downstairs of her husband Alexander Sebastian (Claude Rains). Eventually he does leave the party and the actions in the two locations do converge, as Sebastian goes down to the cellar to get more champagne and sees a passionate kiss between his wife and "the other man." The alternation of action shots that threaten to intersect produces suspense. Every one of Hitchcock's films uses extended crosscutting sequences in this way.

Essential to narrative progression, the flashback is used almost exclusively in fiction films. The **flashback** is a narrative sequence that interrupts the present by a shot or a series of shots representing the past. It is usually announced by a dissolve which, by keeping both time periods on the screen together, visually unites the past and the present. In *Casablanca*, one scene begins with a close-up of Rick's face as he exhales smoke from his cigarette. The smoke softens the focus and covers the dissolve that moves the location into the next slightly soft-focus shot of the Arch of Triumph in Paris. The focus sharpens as Rick and Ilsa drive into the foreground. Now in the flashback, Rick's memory moves forward by means of several overlapping, rather slow dissolves that collapse time so that the dissolves could be spanning hours, days, or months. The flashback ends with another dissolve through smoke, this time from the train to Marseilles which is moving from screen left to screen right. The camera pans from left to right, going back to Rick at his table drinking in the "present." The end of the sequence is punctuated by the sound of the breaking glass that Rick, in his pain at the memory, knocks over. In *Casablanca*, the flashback explains Rick's present circumstances. In *Stand By Me*, the flashback contains the whole story introduced by the dissolve at the beginning and the narrator's voice-over. *Citizen Kane* is entirely based on a series of flashbacks, each introduced and concluded by a dissolve. The sequence made up of a dissolve leading to a flashback is standard narrative form in classical film.

The **flash forward** does not follow the conventional pattern of the flashback. The "interruption" of the present by the future through daydreams and fantasies is less common than the "interruption" of the past through memories and daydreams. An unusual short science fiction film made by Chris Marker in France, *La Jetée* (1965), uses both the flash forward and the flashback. About time travel and memory, the film moves freely among images of the past, present, and future. Episodes of the television show *Star Trek* and the movie *Star Trek IV* (1987), *Back to the Future* (1985), both of the *Terminator* films (1984 and 1991), and *Twelve Monkeys* (1995), which was inspired by Marker's experimental short, use flashbacks and flash forwards freely since time, in all those films, wraps around itself.

Some filmmakers use minimal editing. British director Mike Leigh constructs his dramas around the scene, instructing his cinematographer to shoot in long takes that capture the actors improvising their dialogue and action. Shooting *Secrets & Lies* (1996) without a script, Leigh filmed the emotional reunion between an adult daughter (Marianne Jean-Baptiste) and her biological mother (Brenda Blethyn) in a single take that runs for approximately eight minutes—no cuts. Unlike Eisenstein, Leigh lets performances, not editing, drive his films.

Whether dealing with a handful or hundreds of individual shots, editing converts them into a connected, coherent, understandable, and often dramatic presentation of information or story. Although narrative films are usually based on a script, the process of editing helps to establish the pace and arranges sequences so as to orient and involve the viewer in an imaginary space and time. If the camera provides the cinema with its visual dimension by imitating a most powerful human eye—looking at objects and people from close up, far away, high above or below—and camera movement provides the physical dimension by imitating a most powerful human body moving freely through locations, then editing provides the intellectual and emotional dimension by imitating the human mind's ability to construct meaning and tell a story.

Chapter 6

Sound

Most people think of film as a visual medium, yet when they are asked about a movie, they often tell the story or repeat snatches of dialogue rather than describe the images. Sometimes the music heard in a film will trigger a memory of the visual images: most moviegoers have had the experience of recognizing a tune even when they do not know its name. But if they have seen the movie, hearing Richard Strauss's *Thus Spake Zarathustra* will doubtless make them think of *2001: A Space Odyssey*. The theme music from *Star Wars*, even if heard in an elevator, causes many people to imagine the characters and scenes set in a galaxy far, far away. Sound—the combination of dialogue, music, and sound effects—is an important part of filmmaking.

Sound has been part of movies for most of film history, so viewers tend to take it for granted. The fact that films were initially silent seems to reinforce the idea that the medium is essentially visual and does not really need sound. But even in the silent era, musicians or narrators provided accompaniment. And almost from the beginning, inventors attempted to find a way to attach sound directly to the picture. Only four years after the birth of movies, Thomas A. Edison was experimenting with ways to synchronize sound and image. As early as 1909, other inventors in the United States and France had moderate success with sound in short films. However, feature-length sound films could not be distributed because of problems with synchronization and amplification. Technological limitations prevented sound film from getting past the novelty stage until the 1920s.

Silent films were never really silent. Just about every movie house had musical accompanists; even the most humble had at least a piano and, usually, a violinist as well. Because selected movies were presented as one act in music halls and vaudeville theaters, musicians, who were participants in the other acts, were readily available to accompany the films. As movies became more popular, exhibitors built theaters specifically designed for them. To make the new medium more respectable, producers began to improve the quality of screenings and wanted music to enhance the films. By 1908 musical scores were being compiled specifically for films, and exhibitors were acquiring grander theaters equipped with full orchestras and magnificent organs to play those scores.

Music was not the only type of sound provided in those early film screenings. Some theaters hired sound effects specialists who would sit in the orchestra pit or behind the screen and create sounds—thundering hooves, gunshots, rain drops—at appropriate moments in the movie. Special sound-effects machines such as the Noiseograph and the Excelsior Sound Effect Cabinet were developed. Sometimes a Master of Ceremonies acted as a live commentator who explained the film, told the story, spoke dialogue for one of the characters, or gave details about the film's production. Companies of actors sprang up who specialized in presenting dialogue from behind the screen. Sound was a concern long before technology made synchronous sound-on-film possible (see fig. 47).

Why was the coming of sound in 1927 so significant? That was the year a reliable sound system made the "talkie" possible. Before Al Jolson delivered the historic line "You ain't heard nothin' yet" in *The Jazz Singer*, sound was provided through live performance, and, therefore, both expensive and unpredictable. Technicians were frustrated by their inability to reproduce the real voices of the actors and the real background sounds of life to support the illusions of reality that had been created. Ultimately, inventors developed technology for recording **synchronous sound**, which occurs at the same time as the image producing it, and **asynchronous sound**, which is detached from its source in the film frame.

To be able to record and play back real sound, the visual track and the soundtrack must be perfectly synchronized. To attain synchronization, the sound recording equipment has to record material at exactly the same speed as the camera captures the image. The camera picks up the image at precisely the same time as the microphone picks up the sound. Then the two tracks have to be played back at precisely the same speed. The slightest discrepancy in timing will put the picture out of sync so that lips might visibly mouth one word, while the soundtrack "speaks" the next word; a door might close silently followed a second later by the slam; a

Figure 47. *Saving the Proof.* An enlarged photograph of three frames shows
the sprocket holes on the left and the optical soundtrack on the right of the
16mm film. A photo-electric cell converts sound waves into electric impulses
and electric impulses into light waves, which are then recorded photographi-
cally on the edge of the film strip. The projector's exciter lamp reads these
optical patterns, converting them back to sound.

gangster might pull the trigger of a gun followed a moment later by the
sound of the shot.

The musical comedy *Singin' in the Rain* (1952) provides a humorous
but instructive illustration of the difficulties studios faced during their
conversion to sound. The story is set in 1929, at the beginning of the sound
era, in a Hollywood studio producing its first sound picture. Every possible problem arises. The quality of the heroine's voice is all wrong for
her part. Once dialogue is added, the actors' silent-film style delivery and
broad gestures look too theatrical. The primitive microphone picks up
and magnifies some sounds—the rustle of costumes, the rattle of jewelry,
the clatter of the actors' footsteps—but misses important dialogue. To make
matters worse, the soundtrack slowly goes out of sync until the dashing
hero seems to be speaking the heroine's lines in a shrill, squeaky voice,
while she seems to speak in his deep voice. *Singin' in the Rain* chronicles

the problems that plagued early sound productions. But since the problems were actually overcome rather quickly, the movie survives as an amusing and accurate reminder of the way sound works in film.

In the early days of sound recording, all sound had to be recorded live on the set at the same time. By the early 1930s, directors had learned to mix sync sound with sound recorded elsewhere and add the composite to the images during the postproduction stage (see fig. 48). Freed from the limitations of on-the-spot recording, directors recognized ways to use the new sound techniques to achieve aesthetic goals. For example, in his first sound film *Blackmail* (1929), Alfred Hitchcock gradually had the volume of the dialogue decreased in a scene of a conversation about a murder. The guilty protagonist's terror grows as she (and the audience) hear nearly nothing of the neighbor's chatter except the repeated word

Figure 48. Hallelujah! (d. King Vidor, 1929). Chick (Nina Mae McKinney) dies in Zeke's (Daniel L. Haynes) arms in an Arkansas swamp. King Vidor was the first American director to use post-synchronization, shooting sequences of this film silent with a moving camera, and then later adding sound effects in the studio during the postproduction stage.

"knife"—the murder weapon. Hitchcock manipulated the sound to emphasize the psychological effect of guilt on the young woman, and, at the same time, to convey that feeling to the audience and so increase the drama.

Josef von Sternberg's *The Blue Angel*, made in Germany in 1931, offers another example of inspired use of sound. As the film begins, a maid is busily setting up a breakfast table. She does not speak while she is working, but the audience hears realistic sounds of her activity—doors closing, the coffee pot clinking on the table. She calls her employer to breakfast and, as Herr Rath (Emil Jannings) arrives, the sounds die away, leaving complete silence as he pulls out his chair, pours his coffee, and begins to eat. The sound returns as he whistles over his shoulder. Hearing no response, he gets up and, whistling again, goes over to the bird cage where he finds his pet bird dead. The silence has foreshadowed the canary's death which, in turn, foreshadows the story's tragic ending. In this film, made in the early sound period, von Sternberg has already shifted his emphasis from a purely realistic to a symbolic use of sound.

Just a few years later in *The 39 Steps* (1935), Hitchcock worked out an innovative sound cut. The landlady finds a dead woman's body in Richard Hannay's apartment. The viewer sees the landlady's mouth open to scream but hears the sound of a screeching train whistle instead of her cry, as Hitchcock cuts to a train carrying the fleeing Hannay to Scotland. The cut on the scream-whistle calls attention to the innovative possibilities of sound and, at the same time, moves the story forward in a dramatic way.

Discussing innovations in sound practice is impossible without referring to Orson Welles. Welles came to Hollywood after creating his very successful radio show, *The Mercury Theater.* In 1939, he stunned radio audiences with his broadcast of *The War of the Worlds* by fabricating a "news report" on the invasion of New Jersey by Martians. Despite several interruptions reminding listeners that they were hearing a fictional story, Welles's use of news reports and sound effects was so realistic that people panicked. The broadcast ended Welles's radio career but opened the door to Hollywood. He took along his extensive experience and applied radio techniques to his first feature.

In *Citizen Kane*, Welles formed a **sound bridge** between shots through the use of a single phrase of dialogue, creating continuity that previously relied only on visual editing conventions. Nearly twenty years pass in the course of two images connected through one line of dialogue. The first shot shows Charles as a young boy opening a Christmas gift from his guardian, Mr. Thatcher, who wishes the child a Merry Christmas. Charles returns the greeting in a defiant tone, "Merry Christmas . . . ." In the next shot, Thatcher speaks the remainder of the wish " . . . and a Happy New Year," in a letter he is dictating to be sent to Charles on the occasion of his twenty-fifth birthday. Through the dialogue, Welles establishes narrative continuity.

Welles was one of the first directors to use sound creatively, including sound on and sound off. **Sound on** is the same as synchronous sound: the sound source is visible in the screen images, like a record player or radio playing the music heard in the shot. **Sound off**, or off-screen sound, adds sounds originating from elements not contained in the frame. Both are used to create an auditory world that enhances and expands upon the visuals. Off-screen sound enlarges the boundaries of the film frame, suggesting people and objects beyond the scope of the image. In the opening scene of Francis Coppola's *Apocalypse Now* (1979), Willard (Martin Sheen) lies on a bed in a hotel room. Sound designer Walter Murch transformed sound on of the ceiling fan above the bed into the sound-off whir of helicopter blades outside the window. Traffic noise and a police whistle—all sound off—are heard as Willard awakens fully and realizes he is still stuck in Saigon, anxiously awaiting instructions for his next mission. The sound design signals Willard's shift in consciousness and reinforces his feelings of being trapped in a hotel room while life goes on in bustling Saigon, and the Vietnam War, represented by the helicopter sounds, escalates in the outside world.

■ Dialogue

Dialogue was even important in silent movies, where printed intertitles appeared on the screen to convey the actors' words and advance the story. Consisting of lines of speech spoken in conversation between two or more characters, **dialogue** defines characters by what they say, how they say it, and by how others respond to their statements. Whether the highly charged language of drama or the amusing remarks of comedy, words make characters believable and establish personality. Dialogue can also have thematic implications.

Not all dialogue occurs on camera, synchronized with the image. The words may be spoken to another character while the listener appears on the screen—perhaps the most common example of off-camera dialogue. The listener's reaction to the words is usually made visible by a physical response on his or her face. Dialogue on and off camera can work together in important ways. Robert Altman, known for his manipulation of sound, developed a style that pays homage to Orson Welles by making use of overlapping dialogue. He has been criticized by producers and critics for having all his actors talk at the same time, thereby making it impossible to understand the dialogue. But Altman has attempted to recreate an extremely realistic atmosphere by reproducing the experience people often have when words are not directed and delivered exclusively to them.

In *McCabe and Mrs. Miller* (1971), Altman overlays dialogue and sound effects. Speakers on and off camera, ambient noise, and conversation appear to be on camera yet never are clearly associated with a specific source. McCabe's words are often difficult to understand, because Altman told Warren Beatty to mumble his delivery. By preventing moviegoers from hearing everything clearly, Altman changes their relationship to the film and requires them to search the image for clues to the dialogue and the narrative. On another level, the theme of the film is the lack of communication. The story is about the relationship between an inarticulate man and an emotionally unavailable woman who prefers to retreat into drug-induced dreams. Their faltering personal communication prevents them from fighting a corporate takeover (see fig. 49).

Figure 49. McCabe and Mrs. Miller (d. Robert Altman, 1971). Warren Beatty and Julie Christie, in the title roles, are in a bar. The film's sound design is characterized by overlapping and indistinct background conversations.

■ Narration

Narration usually means voice-over narration, referring to an off-screen voice that gives information, offers explanation or description, or tells a story. Originally devised for radio plays, narration eventually became a conventional film device. The narrator, usually seen only briefly before becoming a participating character in the story, relates events that she or he has lived through or knows about and which are then seen in flashback. In *Citizen Kane*, the investigative reporter Thompson interviews characters who tell the story of their experiences with Charles Foster Kane. As they speak, their voice-over narration frames each segment. In each case, the narrator and interviewer remain on the screen for a short period until a dissolve shifts the scene to the past being recounted. Each story is told in the first person and ends with another dissolve that returns to the present.

In traditional thrillers and detective films, a voice-over often introduces the protagonist embroiled in complicated events that she or he relates in the first person. *Double Indemnity* (1945), *The Postman Always Rings Twice* (1945), *Murder, My Sweet* (1946), *Out of the Past* (1947), *Sunset Boulevard* (1950), among many others, use this conventional device. The voice-over combined with the dissolve into a flashback continues to be used effectively today. Narrators may participate in the story, as in *Little Big Man* (1970), *She's Gotta Have It* (1986), *The Joy Luck Club* (1993), and *Titanic* (1997), or simply tell a story as in *Fried Green Tomatoes* (1990), or they may remain unseen and disembodied as in *The Age of Innocence* (1993).

Arthur Penn's *Little Big Man* begins with Jack Crabb (Dustin Hoffman), an aged Indian fighter, stating in an interview that he survived Custer's Last Stand. In response to the interviewer's skepticism—because there were no white survivors—he begins to narrate the story of his life. A long flashback opens, and he is not seen again in the present until the end of the film. His voice intervenes from time to time on the soundtrack, usually at significant moments, to comment in hindsight on his youthful adventures. Crabb conducts the story, provides a single point of view, insists on one interpretation and attitude, and controls the viewer's understanding and response.

A self-conscious use of the narrator occurs in *The Princess Bride* (1988), in which a wry old man (Peter Falk) reads a fairy tale to his ailing grandson, and the fantasy images unfold under his voice. As the child worries over the story's outcome or disagrees with its progress, the grandfather's voice interrupts the story. At each interruption the images switch back from the visualized story to the sickroom, where grandfather and grandson argue a bit about the way the narrative should go. When the grandfather returns to the reading, some of the images are "re-run" as he goes back to where he left off, his voice sometimes blending with the voice of a character repeating dialogue within the story. The storybook reading frames the action-adventure that comprises the movie.

In Orson Welles's *The Magnificent Ambersons* (1942), the voice of the narrator (Welles himself) introduces the story and characters in such a way that they respond to his disembodied voice. Once he has set the story in motion, his voice does not intervene again until near the end when he exposes the full significance of the main character's unfortunate situation. Welles's weighty intonations are reminiscent of the all-knowing, Voice-of-God narrators of traditional documentaries and newsreels. The director ends the film with a reflexive or self-referential gesture: after introducing all the actors through cameos, he identifies himself as the narrator but shows only a picture of a microphone—a playful representation of his experience in radio and also of the powerful authorial voice.

In a twist on both the fictional voice-over narrator and the documentary Voice-of-God narrator, the original version of *The Naked City* (1948) begins with the voice of Mark Hellinger, the film's producer, introducing himself as Mark Hellinger, the film's producer. In the course of the story, he talks to the characters (although they do not respond to him), speaks for them, and leaves room for them to speak their thoughts in their own voice-overs. Another version of the powerful author/director figure, Hellinger sets himself up as omniscient, judging the main character's actions and persistently directing the audience's responses. The relation to the documentary narrator reinforces the "truth" of the subject.

In today's documentaries, the disembodied, authoritative Voice-of-God approach has fallen into disfavor, especially among politically sensitive filmmakers. Aware of their potential power as controllers of information, recent documentary filmmakers have avoided the all-knowing narrative voice. Errol Morris's *The Thin Blue Line* (1988) and Michael Moore's *Roger & Me* (1989) deal with issues of narration creatively. Others prefer to let the interviews or live action tell the story, or permit onscreen interviews to become voice-over narration by shifting the images from the speaker to the subject of the interview. Terry Zwigoff's *Crumb* (1994), Errol Morris's *Fast, Cheap, and Out of Control* (1997), and Jehane Noujaim and Chris Hegedus's *Startup.com* (2001) allow the interview subjects to speak for themselves.

There are many strategies in the use of narrative voice. Narrators will always influence interpretation of the images "under" their words by means of the content of their speech: the information they furnish and the details of their tone, accent, and inflection, which, in turn, convey attitude, opinion, and emotion.

■ Music

Except for dialogue, music is the most prevalent type of sound in movies. Music was the original accompaniment to movies and was accepted and expected before sound film even became possible. Asynchronous **background music** underlines an image or carries a mood in fiction films and is as important to the production of meaning as dialogue or narration. In certain cases the music actually functions like narration, imitating the action in a scene and giving information about it. At other times, the music translates emotions, provokes responses, and sets up psychological associations. Is the action suspenseful? Frightening? Terrifying? Romantic? Humorous? Poignant? Nostalgic? Sad? Music cues audiences to a whole range of emotional responses, and that is one reason why movie ads can confidently promise—and deliver—thrills, chills, laughter, and tears.

Composers and musicians know that very slow, fast, high, low, or staccato sounds generate tension, whereas melodic and harmonic music has the opposite effect. Whether writing scores for drama, film, television, or radio, composers have knowingly manipulated certain frequencies of sound to affect audiences in a particular way. For instance, consider the image of a sleeper. The person's expression is calm, the breathing even. Soft music played with that image produces a perfect picture and feeling of tranquillity. A violin added suggests romantic, sweet dreams. A subdued saxophone, instead, might suggest sadness. But bring in the bass and a slow, measured drum beat, and tension increases. Continue to build on the beat, change the melodic violin to a shrill pitch, and the mood suggests a nightmare or the threat of approaching evil. If an image-sound pattern were actually analyzed in this way, the results would have to parallel those of the Kuleshov experiment in editing: the image would remain the same, but this time, because of the shift in the music, the viewer's interpretation of and response to the image would change. Therefore, image and music give meaning to one another.

Music must meet the dramatic needs of the story and fit with sound effects and dialogue. A film's musical score, when mixed with the dialogue and sound effects tracks, becomes integrated with them and with the image. Music is one element in the elaborate sound design created around the images during the postproduction phase.

In the past, certain critics took a theoretical position against "parallel composition" which they saw as the use of music to "repeat" the images. For example, a passionate embrace is seen while romantic music is heard. Those commentators have written in favor of the use of musical **counterpoint**, that is, music and sounds in contrast to the image. Counterpoint makes irony possible. In several films about the Vietnam War, counterpoint is used to comment on the war, even to make a political statement.

In *Apocalypse Now* (1979), American attack helicopters are shown in the sky while Richard Wagner's "Ride of the Valkyries" blasts on the soundtrack. As the helicopters fly over a Vietnamese village, bombing a civilian population that includes women and children, knowledgeable audience members will make the association between Wagner's music and the Nazis. In Stanley Kubrick's *Full Metal Jacket* (1987), the popular songs of the Vietnam War era serve to authenticate the time period. In at least one case, the music also comments on the tragedy of sending young boys into war when, at the end, the soldiers march to the "Mickey Mouse Club" song.

Most music written for or applied to movies underlines and supports the image or creates a mood. This relationship began in the mid-nineteenth century, when the German composer Richard Wagner saw that poetry's use of visual imagery might be extended to music. He created a way of introducing texture into his operas by the use of musical themes. He called these thematic constructions **leitmotifs**, combining the German words *leiten* (meaning to lead or guide) and *motif* (meaning a motive or inner drive, an impulse that causes a person to act in a certain way). Wagner used the term to refer to a short musical phrase that represented a given character, situation, or emotion. Theme and variation recurred, eventually weaving together the entire piece. Silent film musicians, as they accompanied the movies, found the *leitmotif* a handy code to identify individuals, ideas, and personal qualities. Music written specifically for film continued this parallel composition, especially creating atmosphere and mood.

In the German expressionist film *M* (1931), the murderer (Peter Lorre) whistles a fragment of the "Hall of the Mountain King" from Edvard Grieg's *Peer Gynt Suite*. For a time, the audience does not see the murderer, except for his shadow or back, but comes to connect the repeated tune with him. The connection is echoed within the film when a blind street seller, especially sensitive to sounds because of his disability, hears the whistled tune, makes the association, and points out the killer.

Throughout his earlier films, John Ford used music to create tone and mood. He chose musical motifs, usually traditional American hymns sung in scenes by the characters and played as background themes, to underscore the notion of community. Several of Ford's films use the hymn "Shall We Gather By the River" at burials to convey communal strength and unity in the face of death. Musical motifs also establish individual or group identities. In his 1939 classic *Stagecoach*, Ford first accompanies images of the stagecoach on the trail by an upbeat, orchestrated version of "Bury Me Not On the Lone Prairie," emphasizing both the lurking threat of death and the courage to continue the journey. The title sequence introduces the cavalry against the ballad "I Dream of Jeannie with the Light Brown Hair," about a girl left behind in the East. Native Americans, whether on or off screen, are always associated with an ominous drum-beat rhythm that became a cliché of the genre.

In *Little Big Man*, a very different Western made in 1970, one recurrent musical motif is the "Garry Owen" fife-and-drum tune of the United States Cavalry. Director Arthur Penn connects that theme to each of several massacres of Indian women and children. The tune was the Union Army's anthem during the Civil War and is associated with a more gallant cavalry of earlier Westerns. It becomes painfully ironic in this film, underscoring the cruelty and genocide perpetrated against the Native Americans by General Custer's military troops.

Italian director Federico Fellini and Nino Rota worked together through almost all of his films, including *La Dolce Vita* (1960) and *8 1/2* (1963). In *La Strada* (1954), Rota's music influences the viewer's reading of the characters. Gelsomina the clown (Giulietta Massina) learns to play the trumpet in the circus belonging to her brutish employer, Zampano (Anthony Quinn). She learns a simple, melancholy, haunting tune from a whimsical tightrope artist (Richard Basehart), and she plays it again and again throughout the film. At the end, Zampano returns to the town where he deserted Gelsomina and where she very likely died. There he hears the melody sung by a local woman. When he first heard Gelsomina play the tune, he ridiculed it and her. This time the tune brings back the memory of her, and that memory torments him and makes him suddenly feel his loss. Because of the song, in fact through it, Zampano comes to realize he had not valued Gelsomina's simple honesty nor the beauty she brought into his life. This recognition and his suffering make him more human and pitiable to the viewer.

The Italian folk tunes that inspired Rota in the early Fellini films and the simple American hymns and folk songs used extensively by John Ford stand in contrast to the lush, rich, romantic, European-style compositions of Miklós Rózsa, Bernard Herrmann, and Max Steiner who composed music during the 1940s and 1950s for Hitchcock, Welles, and the directors of the *film noir* thrillers. The composers' music cues the audience to emotions the scene intends to create and at the same time helps to generate those emotions: suspense or romance or hope.

For *Psycho*, Bernard Herrmann wrote background music that, together with symbolic elements, narrative structure, and sound effects, sets up a complex association between Norman Bates and birds. The connection runs through the whole film: the murdered woman's surname is Crane and she lives in Phoenix; she chats with Norman one night in a room decorated with stuffed birds; when she begins to eat the snack he has prepared for her, he tells her she eats like a bird. Visually, many subtle references pertain to birds including Norman's bird-like motions, framed pictures of birds, and the use of mounted birds as framing devices in many shots. The soundtrack extends the association when the music, ambient

Figure 50. Psycho. Norman (Anthony Perkins) is horrified by what his "mother" has done. The film builds the bird motif through sound and visuals. Norman's posture, his claw-like hand over his mouth, the shape of his jacket, and the wing-like shadow of his arm on the wall echo the picture of the bird behind him.

sound, dialogue, sound effects, and silence work together to continue the bird motif and generate suspense (see fig. 50). When Norman invites Marion Crane into his parlor for a bite to eat, only realistic noises are heard during their conversation. But when she casually suggests that he consider putting his invalid mother "someplace," he is horrified and enraged. His voice rises as he demands: "You mean an institution? A madhouse?" At that moment, very low-pitched music with a repeating beat and a vio-

Figure 51. Psycho. In the famous shower sequence, Marion Crane (Janet Leigh) screams, the sound merging with the high-pitched, bird-like shrieking of violins on the soundtrack.

lin begins and continues quietly until Marion rises to leave; the music suddenly stops. When she leaves to return to her room, the throbbing music resumes with a steady violin that becomes increasingly insistent and high-pitched during the next two transitional scenes. Then comes the shower scene.

At first only natural sounds are heard: the shower curtain being pulled closed and the steady sound of water running. Several dramatic and varied camera angles show Marion showering, looking happy in her decision to return the stolen money. Subtly the editing cuts to a shot that shows, through the shower curtain, the bathroom door beginning to open. Suddenly the sound of the shower curtain pulled back is heard, followed immediately by a high-pitched shriek of the violins on the soundtrack. Marion's scream merges with the bird-like rhythmical screams of the violins (see fig. 51), which continue as she is repeatedly stabbed, until she is dead, and the killer has run off. The alternation of low-pitched music, high-pitched violins mixed with realistic sounds, and silence creates and sustains suspense. Later the high-pitched, bird-like shrieks of the violins are repeated and mark the brief scene of the murder of Detective Arbogast. The bird-like sounds, added to the bird's-eye shot and a hawk-like, downward-swooping motion of the attack, strengthen the bird motif.

Throughout *Psycho*, beginning with the titles and especially in the two murder sequences, the music is an important thread in the intricate fabric of the film. The murder in the shower consists of about seventy-five cuts in a few seconds of screen time. The editing and content of the shots shock the viewer. The sound is as powerful as the images in provoking anxiety and suspense, magnifying and intensifying the viewer's responses.

Well-known popular songs are also used to enhance image, theme, and story. Many period pieces, films set in a specific historical moment, rely on songs of the time to give authenticity to the film. George Lucas made *American Graffiti* in 1972. Wanting to recreate the late 1950s and early 1960s of Modesto, California, his home town, he insisted on the cars, clothes, hairstyles, and slang of the period. The single most important element, the one that gives the true feel of the era, is the rock-and-roll music on the soundtrack. The popular songs, sometimes coming from the car radio and sometimes from off-screen sources, provide the background to the cruising, dating, fighting, and dancing necessary to the believable portrayal of the lives of the characters. The song lyrics also offer a subtle running commentary.

In two semi-autobiographical films, Woody Allen's *Radio Days* (1986) and Neil Simon's *Brighton Beach Memoirs* (1987), the music of the 1930s defines stories of growing up during the Great Depression. Films set in the more recent past use appropriate songs, in some cases to recreate a specific year: *The Right Stuff* made in 1983 is set in 1956; for *Back to the Future* made in 1985, it is 1955; for *The Ice Storm* made in 1997, it is 1973. Each story relies on the popular songs of the depicted year to orient and remind the viewer of the times.

A new musical trend mixes contemporary songs with movies taking place in the distant past. *A Knight's Tale* (2001), a medieval adventure set in the 1370s, stages jousting matches to the music of Thin Lizzy, War, and Bachman-Turner Overdrive. Nicole Kidman sings "Diamonds Are a Girl's Best Friend," Christina Aguilera, Lil' Kim, Mya, and Pink reinterpret La Belle's "Lady Marmalade," and Ewan McGregor belts the Elton John ballad "Your Song" in *Moulin Rouge*, a 2001 release intentionally filled with anachronisms. Although the songs are from the wrong time period, the lyrics contribute to the character and story development and the music fits the mood.

The major importance of music lies in its capacity to produce meaning. In narrative features, music functions as background and support to the image and is as important to meaning in film as dialogue or sound effects. Music can anchor the significance of the image, intensify its emotional qualities, comment ironically, and foreshadow events in the story.

■ Sound Effects

Sound effects refer to all sounds that are not dialogue, narration, or music—everything from the tweet of a bird or the slam of a car door to the most fantastic creations of the supernatural and the extra-terrestrial. One source of sound effects is a stock library where sounds are stored on CD. Some are recorded during production, when the sound recorder tapes dialogue, effects, and ambient sound. Other effects are looped in a studio by foley artists who watch projected sequences and create the appropriate sounds for them at the same time. Whether effects are recorded live or created by electronic or mechanical devices, a great deal of artistry, craft, thought, and care go into their fabrication and use.

Producing sound effects has become so complex over the years that it requires specialists called **sound designers**. Real noises, captured by a microphone, do not necessarily sound like a viewer's experience or expectation of them. For example, one sound engineer explained that recording ocean waves breaking on a beach results in a hissing sound rather than a crashing roar. Waves can be more convincingly produced by spraying water from a large hose onto gravel. Movie audiences accept noises they have never heard or noises that sound different in life. The most obvious examples are sounds of a gunshot or a fistfight. In an open street a real gunshot makes a popping sound, not the deafening blast produced by Dirty Harry's .44 Magnum on the streets of San Francisco. The dull thuds of a fistfight heard in early sound movies, which may actually be close to the real sounds, have evolved through years of sound engineering into the sharp, cracking smack most filmmakers prefer for dramatic effect. The sound designer has the task of either enhancing some noises so they sound more realistic than the real thing or entirely fabricating them when there is no "real thing" — such as light sabers or photon torpedoes in science fiction films.

Most sounds need processing. The most common method is to distort a sound by slowing it down or speeding it up, thereby altering its pitch. Today digital editing technology makes this easy to do: a sound editor feeds a sample of a sound into a computer that can then manipulate it and provide a whole range of sounds from the one originally recorded. **Digital processing** can also combine layers of sounds from different sources. Ben Burtt's first task as the sound designer for *Star Wars* (1977) was to create the voice of a Wookie. He recorded the sounds of a bear, which supplied the base for the Wookie's speech. Then Burtt sweetened that with the barks, growls, and whimpers of dogs, lions, and walruses to complete Chewbacca's voice.

When Ron Bochar created the sound effects for FBI agent Clarice Starling's (Jodie Foster) first interview with imprisoned killer Dr. Hannibal Lecter (Anthony Hopkins) in Jonathan Demme's *Silence of the Lambs*

(1991), he "stacked" several layers of sound effects. To create a horrifying prison ambiance, he added animal and human howls. Then he took a track of screaming from *Little Monsters*, a movie he had worked on two years before, and processed it—slowing it down, playing it in reverse, and integrating the low sound into the prison room tone. The result is subtle yet effective.

During the **mix**, all tracks are adjusted in volume and tonal quality. The director or editor collaborates with the mixer, deciding which sounds must be emphasized to create interest and raise dramatic tension. Such tools as equalizers and filters help blend and balance the sounds created by numerous technicians at different times and places. The complex interweaving of at least forty to sixty tracks during the mix produces associations, emotions, and tension in every film.

The idea that sound derives from and serves the image is changing. Soundtracks of the 1930s and 1940s shared a single invisible loudspeaker or a cluster of speakers that reproduced the same sound at the same time from the same spot behind the screen. Today sound is no longer hidden behind the image. Most theaters have six separate sound channels: center, front (left and right), side surround (left and right), and subwoofer. The original Dolby Surround Sound system, which made its debut with *Star Wars* in 1977, allowed sound designers to send different effects to different parts of the theater. New digital release formats allow filmmakers to place sounds in the back of the theater as well, thereby expanding space, adding depth, and positioning the viewer within the scene. When the steps of a Tyrannosaurus Rex shake the earth in *Jurassic Park*, subwoofers shake the floors and walls of the theater, while surround speakers envelope viewers in the sound design. The sounds emanating from George Lucas's futuristic, high-speed pod racing vehicles in *Star Wars: Episode 1—The Phantom Menace* come from behind and race over the audience's head—an audio version of 3-D. The movies have become a more sensory, participatory experience.

Real or manufactured, synchronous or asynchronous, sound effects heighten the illusion of reality in film. Sound extends the space of the frame. **Ambient** or **background sound** is not connected to specific visible sources but is necessary to the believability of the world of the story. These sounds evoke and define locations, provide information about place, characters, and actions, and contribute by completing the visual experience.

Real or created sound is a powerful source of meaning. Just as different types of music can change the reading of and response to an image, different sounds can change the mood of an image from ominous to lively to sad to comical to exciting. The sound designer works at a complex task of balancing realism and expressiveness.

Like painters who mix their own colors, filmmakers and their sound designers manipulate sounds until they achieve the desired tones and intensities. While the film industry's realist aesthetic limits the possibility of creating imaginative and expressive sound in movies, music videos (the legacy, perhaps, of the 1960s experimental film movement) have loosened the traditional connections between music and visuals. Through these music videos, many viewers who have not been exposed to experimental films have become familiar with and interested in nonrealistic or even surrealistic images and accept a different connection between those images and music. Through the visual and aural training music videos offer, movies such as *Pink Floyd: The Wall* (1982), *Repo Man* (1984), *Desperately Seeking Susan* (1985), *True Stories* (1986), *Drugstore Cowboy* (1989), *Moulin Rouge* (2001), among others, have become acceptable to a wider audience than was previously considered possible.

Film sound and image must work together to make meaning. The viewer always receives and interprets sounds and relies on them as a guide to reading and responding to the images they accompany.

Chapter 7

Making Meaning

In this chapter we will analyze two narrative films: *Black Rider* (*Schwarzfahrer*, 1992), a short film by Pepe Danquart, and *Little Big Man* (1970), a full-length feature film by Arthur Penn. The structure and meaning of both films will be examined and discussed. Both films are readily available on DVD: *Black Rider* is included in *Short I: Invention*, a collection of award-winning films from around the world, distributed by Time Warner Entertainment (ISBN 0-7907-4733-2).

Black Rider (Schwarzfahrer)

In 1993 German filmmaker Pepe Danquart's *Black Rider* (*Schwarzfahrer*) won an Academy Award in the category of Best Live-Action Short. Although only 12 minutes long, the short film contains all the elements found in the best narrative features. Writer-director Danquart carefully crafted a script that not only engages the viewer through its 3-act dramatic structure, but also makes a strong statement about the subject of racism in Germany and, by extension, anywhere. Through his choice of setting, characters, plot development, symbolism, camerawork, editing, and sound design, Danquart has produced many levels of meaning.

■ Socio-Historical Background

After the Second World War, Germany was divided into East and West sectors and its wartime capital, Berlin, was as well. The western parts developed and grew affluent as the United States helped to rebuild the country. Beginning in the 1950s and continuing into the 1960s, the West German government welcomed so-called "guestworkers" who came in great numbers from their deprived countries—Turkey, Italy, Spain, Portugal, and North Africa, mainly Tunisia and Morocco. These workers took the low-wage menial jobs available in the vital postwar economy of West Germany. In the last four decades, an estimated 8.3 million people have legally emigrated to Germany. They remained there, learned the language, went to school, married, raised families, but, partly because they were visibly distinguishable from native Germans, they were never absorbed into the society. More recently, black Africans from Southern Africa have joined the migration from poor to developed countries.

After the fall of the Berlin Wall in 1989 (fig. 1), reunification of West and East Germany brought the less-affluent East Germans into the job market. Suddenly immigrant groups were seen as competition with workers from within the country in an increasingly scarce market, and foreign workers became targets of violence and hate crimes. Pepe Danquart made *Black Rider* in 1992, when attacks against immigrants by neo-Nazis and Skinheads were on the rise. The Nazi ideology of a "pure Aryan race," dormant for nearly fifty years, was taken up by urban gangs of aimless, hopeless youths, mostly uneducated and chronically unemployed. Nazi ideology fueled and rationalized their violence—shootings, beatings, setting fire to workers in dormitories. These attacks were aimed mainly against Turks, of whom 160,000 of the 2.4 million in Germany live in Berlin, and represent the largest minority group there. At the same time, by 1992 Germany was beginning to confront the realities of a large immigrant population. Laws allowing guestworkers' children born in Germany to become citizens, debated for years, were finally passed in 2000.

In many countries of Western Europe, public transportation functions on the honor system. People are expected to buy tickets and validate them whenever they ride on the streetcars. Ticket Controllers make random checks, heavily fining those who do not show a validated ticket.

■ Plot Synopsis

The film opens at a streetcar stop in Berlin where many people are waiting and finally get on. One of the passengers is a young African black who takes a seat next to an older German woman. She begins a tirade against all foreigners and immigrant groups. The other passengers do not respond. The young man does not react until a Ticket Controller gets on the streetcar checking for paid tickets. At that point the young man suddenly snatches the woman's ticket out of her hand and eats it. She tells the Controller that "the Negro" next to her ate her ticket, but the Controller does not believe her excuse, takes her off the streetcar, and fines her for fare-dodging. The film ends with the streetcar moving on.

■ Film Analysis

Pepe Danquart carefully selected three narrative elements—setting, character, and structure—to produce meaning in *Black Rider*. The action takes place in Berlin, the city once divided by history and politics into east and west sectors, now geographically unified but divided by race, class, ethnicity, beliefs, and age. Berlin is the perfect **setting** for a film dealing with issues of racism and tolerance, since the city itself functions as a literal and figurative symbol of the country's division and subsequent re-unification. Although the Berlin Wall has just come down, some people living there have built psychological walls that prevent the country from coming together. Piece by piece, bigoted attitudes must be dismantled and hate speech must not be tolerated by a silent majority.

Danquart uses Berlin as a **metaphor** for all of Germany, and the streetcar in a similar way. The streetcar contains a diverse group of passengers, who represent a microcosm of the city, and by extension, the country and perhaps Europe. However, the streetcar has an additional function: to take the passengers on a physical and psychological journey in which they must confront their attitudes and decide whether to agree with, ignore, or take action against the statements voiced in their presence.

The journey is an important component of the **initiation archetype**, in which the protagonist attains mature insight through experiences that shape him. This transportation vehicle takes the passengers, and the viewer, to a destination—changing everyone along the way.

Danquart's characters seem realistic. One man reads a newspaper while he waits. A motorcyclist tries to start his bike but fails. An elderly man strolls past a young woman standing at the stop. Two young men talk amiably outdoors, one white and the other the black man who becomes the protagonist. Two young girls whisper and giggle together, one German, the other Turkish. But these **characters** also represent different races, social classes, generations, and philosophical positions. What do the central characters signify?

For the most part, film protagonists and antagonists are defined by what they wear, what they do, what they say, and how others react to them. In **Act One** or the set-up of Danquart's **3-act dramatic structure**, he introduces the viewer to a seemingly content, diverse group of people waiting for transportation. The characters, established in a few shots and in a few minutes, represent a cross-section of contemporary German society: young people, older ones, white, of color, well-dressed and casual. Only one seems upset, the motorcyclist (Stefan Merki) whose bike will not start. The arrival of the streetcar serves as the **catalyst** of the narrative, the incident that puts the story into motion. Everybody, including the motorcyclist who apparently must get to work, piles in. At this point, the viewer does not know who the main characters are or in which direction the plot will turn.

The young black man (Paul Outlaw), wearing jeans and T-shirt and a baseball-type cap, embroidered in a Muslim pattern and worn backwards according to contemporary style, moves into the aisle and stands in front of a woman of a certain age (Senta Moira), rather formally dressed, wearing a hat and coat and make-up. Viewers can see that each of them represents a different race, class, and age. The black (as the end credits refer to him) asks the woman politely—in correct and unaccented German—if the seat next to her is free. She looks him up and down with some disdain, does not answer but does not refuse him. He takes the seat and begins to eat from a pack of nuts. She is visibly irritated by him, pulls her purse away and her coattail out from under him. The seat-selection incident is the first **plot point**, which spins the narrative into a new direction and begins **Act Two**, the confrontation. Now the film has a **protagonist**, the polite black man who takes the seat, and an **antagonist**, the hostile older woman.

At this point, Danquart develops important themes and narrative devices. The director focuses on a little boy (Mark Tiedemann), seated opposite the older woman. He sees her annoyance and smiles conspiratorially at the black guy who responds with a slight smile. The friendly boy displays none of the woman's irritation, instead representing the young generation's acceptance of others. He represents hope for the future of a more tolerant Germany. Danquart contrasts the youth with the older woman, thereby singling her out as a bigot. The camera then cuts to a couple of young Turkish boys (Ali Atmaca and Zozar Atmaca) who flirt with the girls (Anne Trauvetter and Ergin Sari), commenting on their cute looks. The girls look over at the boys and begin to giggle and whisper. The multiracial couples, engaged in friendly chat, and the groups of young people and school children also represent in a positive way Germany's more diverse future.

The second act comprises most of a movie, dealing with the major plot developments that introduce and intensify the conflict. The woman immediately begins a racist tirade that escalates the film's tension. She speaks out loud, first addressing the black man, calling him a "lout" and objecting to his taking the seat next to her, then speaking to no one and to everyone. She complains about "foreigners," her anti-immigrant diatribe covering all groups. She names Italians and Turks, the recent immigrants.

Danquart recognizes that language is the locus of power. Language is the means by which "reality" is constructed. While some words simply describe the world, others shape and reinforce people's perceptions of that world and affect change merely by being spoken. Language that is denigrating creates and reinforces a power gap between speaker and listener. In addition hate speech may incite violent acts. The director defines his antagonist by what she says and positions the viewer against her.

The film introduces another level of meaning as the woman's hate speech extends to the Poles who were not actually among immigrant groups at the time the film was made. Their inclusion references the Second World War when the Nazis defined the Poles as an inferior race, along with Jews and Gypsies.

Black Rider contains hints that the woman might represent past German xenophobia, and her next comments seem to confirm this notion. She accuses immigrants, and specifically the Africans she calls "Hottentots," of causing the country's social problems: unemployment, AIDS, crime. In the 1880s, as a newly-formed country, Germany colonized part of Southwest Africa, now Namibia, but lost the colonies in 1918 after its defeat in the First World War. The local tribe were the Khoikhoin which Dutch settlers to the area called "Hottentots," mimicking the click sounds of their language. The woman uses that pejorative name but the subtitles translate it as "savages." To nineteenth and early twentieth-century Germans, these dark-skinned African tribespeople were the very personification of the "Other." They were primitives, savages, an inferior race. After all, their physical traits were opposite to those the Nazis elevated as perfect: namely, fair-skinned, tall, blond, blue-eyed, Nordic, Aryan. In a single sentence, the woman has reduced African immigrants to lazy, sexually active, diseased, criminal savages.

She also declares that the groups are all "mixing together," worrying that she will not know what country she lives in. This is a code for impurity or "mongrelization" of the races, as the Nazis called it. The woman is old enough to have absorbed notions of German racial superiority and purity, the remnants of Nazi-era beliefs that she represents. By her words, as she names the various ethnic groups, and by her comments on the necessity of keeping people out or making them change their names before coming into Germany, she stands for Germany's Nazi past.

The woman's hate speech drives the narrative in Act Two. She continues and personalizes her attack on the young black man, saying "you smell bad," but "there is no law against it." As she escalates her verbal attack, the camera cuts to the young black man who does not react to her comments, next to the little boy seated opposite them who now looks embarrassed and uncomfortable, and then to other passengers who turn to look but do not intervene, do not confront or challenge her. This marks the **midpoint** of the dramatic structure, usually coming halfway through the film: the protagonist is faced with a big challenge. Will he or anyone stop her? Although the comments are directed against one man, they also deliver a frightening message to any person or to an entire group who may look different or may have different beliefs than the majority. An immediate response to her tirade would promote prevention and awareness. Silence, on the other hand, implies agreement and complicity. No one is teaching the uncomfortable little boy that acts of hate are not acceptable.

Danquart and cinematographer Ciro Cappellari have used traditional filmmaking techniques up to this point, including establishing shots to introduce the setting and orient the viewer within the space. Even their choice of black-and-white film stock seems well suited for a film dealing with race issues. The camerawork and *mise en scène* never call attention to themselves. Simone Brauer's continuity editing also contributes to this illusion of reality: the straight cut, match on action, and eyeline match help render the editing invisible. The spectator is positioned as a detached observer who watches the film from a third-person point of view.

At the midpoint, however, Danquart shifts to a stylized look. He introduces a montage of dissolves, slow motion, and close-ups on eyes to emphasize the moment at which the passengers begin to contemplate their role in the unfolding drama. To situate the spectator within the minds of the passengers, Danquart distorts the sound. This sound design, when combined with intimate camerawork, conveys a sense of the passengers' conflicted thoughts and emotions. The stylistics switch the viewer from a third-person to a subjective point of view and stress the importance of this particular sequence. Midpoints truly challenge the characters, and the **story beats**—the major events in the narrative—begin to happen more quickly. As a result, the viewer becomes more engrossed in the plot, identifies more fully with the protagonist, and cares about the outcome.

The action taken by the protagonist or protagonists at the midpoint usually reveals important character traits. Danquart returns to a realistic style, as though the passengers had snapped out of their musings and made up their minds. One of the young Turkish boys understands the woman's anti-Turkish remark and calls out in Turkish that she does not know what she is talking about, goes on to call her an obscene name, and moves as if to confront her, but his friend says let it go and he backs off. The elderly man seen earlier nods to her in agreement. He has been shown to look disapprovingly at a young man who got on the streetcar, most likely German, with spiky hair and wearing headphones. Most of the other passengers, including the motorcyclist, glance up, look around at her, and go back to their reading, attempting to ignore her. Three different responses are documented: a defensive reaction, support, silence.

These choices encourage the spectator to think about how he or she would react in a similar situation.

The major plot point that begins **Act Three** always speeds the conflict to the climax. The third act begins when the Ticket Controller (Klaus Tilsner) gets on the streetcar to check that all the passengers have paid tickets. The motorcyclist curses, realizing he is about to be caught without a paid fare; from the film's opening scene, his character's purpose has been to set up this situation. The woman pulls out her ticket and, somewhat smugly, holds it in her hand while continuing her attacking monologue. Impassive until then, the black man suddenly whips her ticket out of her hand, puts it in his mouth, quickly chews it up, and swallows it (his eating throughout the trip foreshadows and makes this twist acceptable to the viewer). In the face of the woman's racist words, the black man has had to swallow his anger, but he finally takes action and "punishes" her by swallowing her ticket. The lack of intervention or response by the other passengers stands as a strong critique of German society where some people, like the woman, only speak a right-wing, anti-immigrant ideology, while others, younger and more menacing, like neo-Nazis and Skinheads, act out physical violence.

The only person to see this action, the **climax** of the film, is the little boy. The Controller asks for the tickets. The woman tells him that the Negro (the subtitles incorrectly translate *neger* as "nigger") next to her ate it (*aufgefressen*, devoured). The young black man shows his own ticket, and glances sideways at the woman, lightly suggesting that she is a bit deluded. The Controller thanks him and says he has never heard such a stupid excuse for riding without a ticket. The fact that the Controller, representing government authority, sides with the black man is significant. During the Nazi era, the situation would certainly have been reversed.

In the **falling action**, the Controller escorts the woman off the streetcar, writing her a ticket for traveling without a fare, while she continues to insist that "they now eat our tickets," and that she has never "fare-dodged." The slang expression in German for a fare-dodger is a "black rider." The title thereby gathers multiple meanings: the African black riding on the streetcar is literally a *black rider*; the motorcyclist in a hurry to get on the streetcar is in fact traveling without a paid fare, and so he is a "black rider" or fare-dodger; and the black man turns the woman into a "black rider" when he swallows her ticket.

The film ends with the **resolution**, the streetcar and its passengers moving on towards the center of Berlin—without the person who was spreading hate and intolerance. The protagonist will achieve his goal of arriving at his destination. Although he has not changed during the course of the narrative, he has triggered a new awareness in the other passengers.

The passengers and the viewer, it is hoped, reject the woman's racist convictions, are amused by her comeuppance, and rejoice in her punishment, even though they know that she *did* in fact have a ticket and that the black guy *did* in fact eat it. Since the little boy seated opposite is the sole witness of the black man's action—a question arises of what German children, unconditioned as yet to intolerance, are being taught and what they are learning about race and ethnicity, as well as responsibility. The last words of the film are the woman's appeal to the authority that there were witnesses, that "everyone saw what happened," that "they all saw it." In fact it is true that the passengers, enclosed inside the streetcar, a microcosm of German society, witnessed her statements, did see everything, did hear everything she said, and refused to support her but also refused to stop her.

Although the film has a lighthearted component, it seriously condemns the complicity of the Germans who did not respond in the face of overt bigotry and intolerance, and those who do not take a stand. Made just three years after the fall of the Berlin Wall, *Black Rider* ties together the racism of Germany's Nazi past with the anti-immigrant violence of the time, suggesting that those who cannot remember the past are condemned to repeat it. The film criticizes the silence of the people who are "good, upstanding" folks who most likely do not agree with the woman's expressed racist beliefs, but who do not confront her, challenge her, or stop her. In other words, Danquart is showing that the refusal to take an opposing stand allows crime to flourish. The woman gets her just desserts, but by a clever response, not because of social pressure or a desire for justice by her peers.

Through the interplay among the narrative, visual, and aural elements, Pepe Danquart makes a strong statement against racism and society's weakness as demonstrated by its silence. Combining drama and humor, *Black Rider* exposes contemporary problems and suggests that everyone can make a difference in creating a place where people are free to live and work together, without fear of intolerance or hatred.

Little Big Man

Arthur Penn's *Little Big Man* (1970) is a useful film to examine for an analysis of meaning. The film is a **Western** and, like others, is set in the post-Civil War period during the great westward expansion that took place between 1865 and 1890. Few Westerns are complete without a conflict between Indians and whites, and *Little Big Man* is no exception. Whereas classic Westerns portray the whites as representatives of civilization and the Indians as barbarians, this one suggests the opposite. The Indians are victims of malevolent treatment by the United States Army, which, using a highly developed technology against innocent and peaceful natives, took the land and food sources and destroyed the indigenous culture.

To convey this revisionist view of the effects of westward expansion on Native Americans, the film's narrative structure combines elements from two literary traditions: the **picaresque** (in which the roguish hero encounters a series of adventures) and the **initiation archetype** (the hero attains mature insight through experiences that shape him). Like other youthful hero figures, Jack Crabb, the protagonist of *Little Big Man*, is initially innocent and ignorant, but through his exposure to both white and Cheyenne cultures, he develops and learns and is able to choose between them. The film presents this structure of initiation and transformation in a comic and ironic narrative that demythologizes famous legendary figures, the Western hero, and the Indians. The fusion of cinematic elements—the generic reversals, the parodic tone, the narrative structure, the representation of Native Americans—makes *Little Big Man* unique and worthy of study. To analyze the film for meaning, the viewer must examine the way symbols and motifs evoke larger themes based on universal, cultural, and textual connotation.

■ The Western Film

Some silent films, D.W. Griffith's *The Massacre* (1912) and James Cruze's *Covered Wagon* (1923), offered a tolerant portrayal of Indians. But by the 1930s and 1940s, Hollywood Westerns reinforced images and stereotypes of Native Americans that had evolved during the previous century. These relied almost entirely on the figure of the bloodthirsty warrior whose hostile actions and threatening presence impeded the taming of the West. This conception of American history began to shift slightly in the 1950s when a variation arose in the genre. Several directors made Westerns that showed Native Americans badly treated by the white man: swindled by greedy white traders in Stuart Gilmore's *The Half-Breed* (1952) or provoked into battle by hateful cavalry officers in Sam Fuller's *Run of the Arrow* (1956). Delmer Daves's *Broken Arrow* (1950), Anthony Mann's *Devil's Doorway* (1950), and Robert Aldrich's *Apache* (1954) also introduced a positive representation of Indians. Native Americans (portrayed by white actors) are central characters who are honorable and brave, yet targets of racism.

In the early 1960s, several major releases brought this more sympathetic view of Indians to mainstream audiences. Don Siegel's *Flaming Star* (1960) focuses on the plight of a "half-breed," a mixed-race son of a white father and Indian mother, who is the blameless object of prejudice. Then John Ford, a major filmmaker largely responsible for the stereotypical view of the savage Indian, directed *Cheyenne Autumn* (1964). Ford modified the negative portrayal of the Native American in his previous Westerns by depicting the heroism of the Cheyenne people as they attempted under terrible conditions to trek a thousand miles on foot back to their homeland. The film shows the dignity of the Indians in the face of the United States government's harsh and unfair military policy toward them. Martin Ritt's *Hombre* (1967) and Sydney Pollack's *The Scalphunters* (1968) continued this sympathetic attitude toward Native Americans, reevaluating Hollywood's representation of the Indian.

■ Socio-Historical Background

Little Big Man, adapted from Thomas Berger's novel of the same title, was released in the winter of 1970. The differences between Berger's book, written in 1964, and Calder Willingham's final script illustrate the shift in social attitudes that had occurred during those years. The novelist's fanciful parody of the Old West ridicules all the characters—the Indians, the white settlers, the United States Cavalry, as well as the legendary figures of Wild Bill Hickck and General George Armstrong Custer. It also challenges the credibility of the main character and narrator, Jack Crabb. Is he the frontier's most overlooked hero or the biggest liar to set foot on the Great Plains? The screenplay, on the other hand, makes Jack Crabb entirely sympathetic and believable, and thoroughly committed to the Indian cause. This characterization propels the narrative into a passionate protest against the treatment of Native Americans.

During the mid-to-late 1960s, the escalating war in Vietnam, along with the emerging civil rights, feminist, ecology, and American Indian movements, dominated the public discourse and affected the content of many films. A growing antiestablishment mood reflected the disappointment felt by many Americans, especially the young, whose dreams and ideals were dashed by the assassinations of John F. Kennedy, Martin Luther King, Jr., Robert Kennedy, and Malcolm X. Films first signaled a shift in cultural values when offbeat protagonists and counterculture themes emerged in *Bonnie and Clyde* (1967), *The Graduate* (1969), and *Butch Cassidy and the Sundance Kid* and *Easy Rider* (both 1969). *Little Big Man* was produced during the political and social turmoil of this era, and reflected the consciousness of the movements of the time, the social attitudes they generated, and an overall criticism of America's morality and values.

Changes in the American film industry made it possible to express the disillusionment and growing cynicism of a good part of the population. The breakdown of the studio system and the increasing prestige and influence of European art films encouraged independent film production and production of movies targeted to specific markets, especially, and for the first time successfully, the youth market. In addition, the elimination of the Production Code in 1968 permitted the depiction of graphic violence and sex on the big screen. The films produced as a result of these factors dared to offer nontraditional themes in nontraditional cinematic formats. By the end of the decade, mainstream films had begun to reflect the themes and experiences of the counterculture.

■ Plot Synopsis

Little Big Man opens with Jack Crabb (Dustin Hoffman), now 121 years old and in a Veterans Administration hospital, talking into an interviewer's tape recorder. He introduces himself as "the sole white survivor of the Battle of the Little Big Horn, popularly known as Custer's Last Stand" and tells his story (which begins in the 1850's), relates the "facts" of his life, and periodically comments on these events in a voice-over. His experiences unfold in a flashback: a Cheyenne brave (Ruben Moreno) brings ten-year-old Jack to his tribe after the Pawnee kill the boy's family in a raid. Adopted by the Cheyenne Chief, Old Lodge Skins (Chief Dan George), Jack lives with them until his late teens and learns their tribal customs, language, and philosophy of life and moral order. The tribe names him "Little Big Man" because, although he is physically small, he gained stature by saving the life of a fellow brave, Younger Bear (Cal Bellini).

During a skirmish between the Cheyenne and the U.S. Cavalry, a soldier captures Little Big Man and places him in the home of a Baptist minister, the Reverend Pendrake (Thayer David) and his wife (Faye Dunaway). From them, Jack receives a white man's education and Christian moral training. He becomes aware of their hypocrisy and leaves them, disillusioned, when he discovers Mrs. Pendrake in a tryst with her lover. Jack tries various frontier occupations, each of which requires him to change his identity and acquire new skills. However, once again disillusioned by the failure of his undertakings, he moves West with his Swedish wife, Olga (Kelly Jean Peters). On the way, Indians attack the stagecoach and kidnap her. Jack sets out to find his wife, but his former brothers capture him and return him to the tribe. Wanting to continue his search for Olga, he leaves the Indian village and attaches himself to General George Armstrong Custer's (Richard Mulligan) Seventh Cavalry. After he sees the regiment slaughter an entire encampment of Indian women and children, he deserts and returns once again to the Cheyenne. A happy period with an Indian wife (Amy Eccles) follows, but ends when, during another massacre led and encouraged by Custer, he watches a soldier kill his wife and newborn son.

At this point Jack longs to assassinate Custer but is unable to do so and, ashamed of his weakness, turns to drink (see fig. 52). Alone, disheveled

Figure 52. *Little Big Man* (d. Arthur Penn, 1970). Jack Crabb (Dustin Hoffman) has sunken into dissolution in white society. He is literally and figuratively in the gutter.

and on the verge of suicide, he catches sight of Custer's regiment on the move, and decides he must "look the devil in the eye and send him to Hell where he belongs." At the Little Big Horn, Custer asks Jack, now his scout, whether to attack or retreat. Jack knows that thousands of Indians from many tribes have assembled there to battle the white man, sees the opportunity to send Custer to his certain death, and challenges him to attack. Custer, thinking Jack is trying to outwit him and wanting to outwit Jack, leads his troops into the ravine of the Little Big Horn. In the famous battle of June 25, 1876, Custer and his entire regiment are, of course, annihilated. However, Jack is saved by his old rival Younger Bear who returns him to the decimated Cheyenne tribe.

Old Lodge Skins foresees the end of the Cheyenne and readies himself for his own death. When his preparations fail, the Chief, stoical and good humored, recognizes life's inevitable ironies and remarks: "Sometimes the magic works; sometimes it doesn't." The flashback ends with this scene, and the film concludes with a return to the hospital where Crabb dismisses the interviewer who, like the viewer, has been surprised and humbled by this narrative.

■ Film Analysis

Little Big Man combines the two literary forms of the picaresque and the initiation archetype. It shares the satirical tone and episodic plot of the picaresque tradition. It also shares the character development and dramatic structure of the initiation archetypal pattern: the hero's formation and growth, his journey from ignorance and innocence to wisdom and maturity. Jack Crabb attains maturity and insight through his contact with white and Cheyenne societies.

Jack's journey as hero opens his eyes to contrasting values. The whites of frontier society are hypocritical, goal-oriented, and exploitative. Unable to accept the values he sees driving white civilization—hypocrisy, greed, lust for power and money—Jack moves through phases, increasingly disillusioned. He first discovers that people in white society say one thing and do another, often the opposite. Mrs. Pendrake, the minister's wife, pretends to be a pure, God-fearing, respectable woman but behaves sinfully. Mr. Pendrake pretends to be a man of God, yet visibly relishes the thought of beating religion into young Jack. General Custer seems, at a distance, to be great and noble, but up close emerges as a megalomaniacal, tyrannical, arrogant madman.

Mirrors function as a textual symbol to convey the two-faced hypocrisy of white civilization and its immense regard for appearances. Characters repeatedly examine themselves in mirrors as though checking to see if they fit the part they have chosen to play. Mrs. Pendrake's lover smoothes his mustache while looking into a small hand mirror in which he sees her walk into his store. The snake-oil salesman, Mr. Merriweather (Martin Balsam), primps in front of a little mirror outside of his tent just before he and Jack are tarred and feathered and run out of town. Jack sees the reflection of Wild Bill Hickok (Jeff Corey) in a barroom mirror before he sees the man—a fitting introduction to a myth.

And Custer, after Jack fails to kill him, sits before a mirror calmly trim-ming his mustache. After Jack discovers Mrs. Pendrake with her lover, he, too, now a part of that society, studies himself in a mirror as though to register the deep change in him caused by the experience. Vanity is everywhere among this group: appearances are more important than substance, reflections supplant reality.

In each phase of Jack's initiation, he learns a lesson while searching for identity and trying to fit into society's mold. When his religious pe-riod ends in the discovery of hypocrisy, he reacts by entering his snake-oil salesman period, but he is too honest. Reunited with his sister Caroline (Carol Androsky), he learns from her how to shoot and enters his gun-fighter period, but he is sickened when Wild Bill Hickok shoots a man in cold blood. Unable to kill just to build a reputation, he becomes a store-keeper, but his partner cheats him and he loses everything. In every stage, Jack learns that to succeed in white society he must take advantage of others.

In contrast, the Indian way of life emphasizes harmony. Individuals grow older, some are killed—often by the white man—but new families are formed, and the tribe moves across the land according to the natu-rally changing seasons. The Cheyenne express their feelings honestly and accept differences: they tolerate their fellows, including the Contrary who does everything backwards and the *heemaneh* who, although male, lives as a woman.

By portraying the Cheyenne as natural, unaffected, honest, generous, and accepting, the film asserts that life among the whites is the opposite: artificial, deceitful, fraudulent, greedy, and intolerant. In contrast to the Indians' recognition of a center to life, a moral and spiritual essence around which all things revolve and which gives meaning and balance to existence, whites "do not know where the center of the earth is," as the old chief says. The Cheyenne consider the cycles of time, seasons, and days to be part of the great circle of life. This concept is important in many Indian cultures and is used in the film as a strong visual and thematic element: teepees are built on a circular plan, the Indian camp is circular in arrangement, and many artifacts are based on a circular design. At one point, Little Big Man convinces his grandfather to escape an attack only by persuading him that he must flee to the river, which, he reminds the old man, "is part of the great circle of the waters of the earth." The har-monious, cyclical nature of the Cheyenne ways, embodied in the motif of the circle, contrasts visually to the activities of the whites, which are either rigidly linear (regiments of marching soldiers) or destructively chaotic (the massacres).

While the Indians are shown to be innocent victims, the whites are shown to be swindlers, cheats, and racist killers. Desperate for financial success, they succumb to restless dissatisfaction, refuse all social checks or limits, and behave viciously. The moral bankruptcy of white American society is another primary theme of the film and is developed through the motif of the massacre. Through repetition of the scenes of attack by the United States military on the Indian women and children, screenwriter Willingham and director Penn set out to expose the myth of the westward expansion and to present the hidden side of the historical record, including the systematic murder and brutal resettlement of Native Americans in the nineteenth century. When Custer says with nearly hysterical hatred and contempt that the Indian women "breed like rats," he clearly means (and is understood to mean) that they must be exterminated like rats. Custer's personal malice hides policy issues: not coincidentally, the result of the genocide is appropriation of their land. The whites' drive for money and power blends with a racism that, for them, justifies the slaughter of the Indians.

Little Big Man also resonates with issues that divided this country in the late 1960s. For movie audiences of the time, enmeshed in the controversy over American military intervention in Vietnam, the film's images of innocent people being slaughtered by ruthless soldiers made strong reference to the just-published newspaper accounts of the criminal massacre of civilians at My Lai, carried out months before by Army Lt. William L. Calley, Jr., and some of his troops. The information emerged in shocking headlines in November 1969 as shooting on the film was being completed.

Forthright as the filmmakers were on the issues of racism and military aggression, they were considerably less progressive in their narrative treatment of women and alternative lifestyles and behaviors. Film roles for women have usually been stereotypical, with women's real concerns and plight either mocked or ignored. *Little Big Man* is no exception. Although Jack Crabb and his grandfather, Old Lodge Skins, are clearly the only fully developed characters in the film, the male secondary characters emerge as individuals. Custer's vanity and egotism are as neatly drawn as his racism. Merriweather is so careless with himself in his drive for success that each time he appears, he is missing a hand, a leg, or an eye. Among the Cheyenne braves, Shadow-Who-Comes-Inside and Younger Bear are individuals, each with his own personality and qualities.

The women characters are only stereotypical foils. Jack's sister Caroline "wants" to be raped by the Indians and as a result of their "rejection," turns into a man-hater. Mrs. Pendrake, married to a straitlaced preacher, is sketched as a sexually avid woman, unfaithful, seductive, and lusting after Jack, her foster son. She is last seen, having fallen on bad days, as a prostitute. Olga is the typical middle-class wife, who, once stolen by the Indians, becomes a shrew and bosses her Indian husband. The depiction of the Cheyenne women suggests a Sixties stereotype: they personify the "natural" women of the era who engaged in communal living and practiced sexual freedom. The film introduces Sunshine courageously giving birth in hiding while soldiers slaughter her people in a nearby encampment. Later she goes off alone like a wild creature to deliver her second child. Subsequently portrayed as a coy child-wife, unhampered by puritanical hang-ups about monogamy and fidelity, Sunshine insists on sharing her husband with each of her three sisters, who are, in turn, more than willing collaborators. A scene of communal lovemaking in the teepee mirrors the image of a hippie commune and reflects the free-love, open-marriage ethos associated with the Sixties. The treatment of women and their issues is negligible here as elsewhere in Hollywood feature films.

As a group, the Indians represent the Sixties counterculture and its return to nature, communal living, experimentation with alternate lifestyles, and tolerance for others. Nevertheless, although Jack reports in his voice-over narration that the tribe admires and respects Little Horse (Robert Little Star), the *heemaneh*, the film encourages the spectator to ridicule him. The movie draws him as an affected, homosexual stereotype: he takes on mannerisms such as fluttering his eyelashes, dancing flirtatiously, and lisping coy lines of dialogue. The tribe also accepts Younger Bear's (Cal Bellini) behavior as a Contrary without casting judgment on him. Because Younger Bear does everything backwards and acts outrageously for no explained reason, he appears angry, crazy, and bizarre to the viewer. Through this portrayal, the film evokes the outlandish, drug-induced behavior associated with the Sixties.

Even though *Little Big Man* pokes fun at the Indians and at the counterculture, the film indicates the serious losses experienced in the 1960s. Jack Crabb's grief over the tragic fate of the Native Americans becomes emblematic of the nation's lament over the assassinations; the extinction of cultures, species, and habitats; and the pollution and devastation of the environment. American youth recognized that the Indian way of life, deeply spiritual and ecologically sound, was a model that modern society had ignored. They took up these causes in the political and social arena, noting the harmony of Native American ways, as they searched for meaning and purpose in their own lives. Jack tells his story to preserve the Cheyenne heritage and also to offer lessons for America in 1970. Indeed *Little Big* Man struck such a deep chord in young audiences that it became the second highest domestic box-office hit of that year.

■ Sequence Analysis

How are these abstract meanings conveyed? A detailed examination of a single sequence shows how it contributes to the creation of the themes and motifs of the film. The sequence occurs early in the film, immediately after the young Jack Crabb has become the Cheyenne warrior "Little

Big Man." At the end of the naming ceremony, an integral element in the ritual of initiation, a cut moves the scene to the small band of Indians traveling across the plains. The scouts suddenly catch sight of smoke on the horizon, so they ride off to investigate.

Description: The braves ride into the middle of an Indian encampment that has been burned and is still smoldering. Only the teepees' frames remain. The bodies of the Indian inhabitants and debris are scattered everywhere. The camera holds on the corpses of several children and women. In a medium shot, Little Big Man says to Old Lodge Skins, "I don't understand it, Grandfather. Why would they kill women and children?" The old man replies, "Because they are strange . . . ." The camera, tilting down, pauses on an army saddlebag lying on the ground with the letters "US" stenciled on it. He continues, "They do not seem to know where the center of the earth is." The camera cuts from shot to shot of the dead Indians. The next shot shows one of the Cheyenne braves who has returned from an investigation of the whole area. In sign language, he reports that everyone is dead. The old man says: "We must have a war on these cowards and teach them a lesson." Cut to the next sequence as the Cheyenne prepare for battle with the Cavalry.

Literal Meaning: The women and children of an entire Indian village have been annihilated, and the saddlebag reveals who the perpetrators are. The chief states that the reason the soldiers have massacred the village is the white man's failure to be at peace with nature. He decides to retaliate "to teach the cowards a lesson."

Connotative Meaning: Between the seventeenth and nineteenth centuries, Americans learned two contradictory myths about Indians. One, deriving from the Puritan fear of the uncontrolled wilderness and its inhabitants, depicted Native Americans as bloodthirsty savages. The other flourished in the writings of eighteenth-century European Romantics and presented Indians as noble savages, living in an unspoiled wilderness and spiritually pure. Both these views were perpetuated in America in the nineteenth-century novels of James Fenimore Cooper. In *The Pioneers*, *The Last of the Mohicans*, *The Prairie*, *The Pathfinder*, and *The Deerslayer* — all five collected in *The Leatherstocking Tales* — Indians were wild, ferocious, and uncivilized, but also brave, dignified, proud, and wise teachers. These contrasting ideas about Indians are part of American culture and allow most viewers to accept movies in which scantily dressed men with feathers in their hair ride wildly out of ravines, ready to kill, brandishing spears, and shrieking at the top of their lungs. But viewers can also accept a calm, wise elder, a weathered Indian chief in full-feathered headdress, speaking in poetic words of wisdom about life and nature.

The sequence under examination presents cultural myths indirectly through setting, character, and circumstances. The transitional shots that lead into this sequence show the Cheyenne moving across the plains. In the foreground, buffalo graze placidly, undisturbed by the presence of the Indians. The shot suggests that Indian and buffalo share the land and are part of a harmonious balance of nature. This sequence contrasts to a later scene of white buffalo hunters stacking huge piles of skins, visually emphasizing the rapacious nature of those who kill the buffalo not for sustenance but for financial gain.

The first shot of the sequence shows the small figures of the Indians, quite insignificant in a wide expanse of yellow grassland as they ride off to investigate dark smoke in the distance. The open spaces offer little protection, and along with the small size of the group on the spacious land, the shot suggests their vulnerability, their supreme self-confidence, and their courage in the face of possible danger. These perceptions are reinforced by the next shot of the burned-out Indian village, followed by a closer look at the destruction of this Indian camp. The camera holds on the image of dead women and children in the encampment, a powerful image in view of the social, moral, and cultural taboo against the killing of civilians even in war. The fire is smoldering; only tent frames and tattered, smoking remnants remain, implying that the immediate danger is past but also that there has been a massacre: bodies are sprawled randomly, the people caught unawares and in the middle of their daily routine. The controversy over American activities in Southeast Asia made these images a strong reference, for movie audiences of the time, to the killing and maiming of women and children in Vietnam.

Old Lodge Skins, previously established as wise and moral, quietly comments on the scene. His troubled and thoughtful expression, and his stylized and lyrical speech contribute to his image as sage—the personification of the noble Indian. The representation of Old Lodge Skins and the Cheyenne are as idealized and as mythicized as were the heroic cowboys and gunfighters in classic Westerns. For example, Penn and art director Dean Tavoularis selected muted tones for the Indian clothing in order to visually reinforce the harmonious association between the Native Americans and the earth. The contrast in this sequence between the serenity of the Cheyenne and the atrocities they have witnessed introduces the theme of an intolerant and brutal white society out of balance with nature.

Textual connotation arises from the repetition of certain elements in a film text. The close shot of the burned Indian village in this sequence introduces the textual motif of the circle, which is repeated in the shape of the nearby pond and in the shields and artifacts belonging to the group. The circle is a universal symbol representing harmony, wholeness, and unity, all of which are connected to the Indians. The point is that the soldiers, "who do not know where the center of the earth is," have destroyed the teepees and with them, the circle. Because they are not centered themselves, the soldiers willfully destroy the dwellings and their inhabitants. That destruction adds to the larger moral contrast between the whites and the Indians.

Why are the dead bodies in the village emphasized? The bodies are the concrete visual symbol representing the massacre, another textual motif that develops the theme and creates emotional impact. The motif explodes the myth that the westward expansion was entirely heroic and unsullied, and exposes the historical realities of the nineteenth-century genocide of Native Americans. The film's pre-title sequence introduces the motif: the historian interviewing the ancient Jack Crabb says, with an embarrassed laugh, that the American treatment of the Indians bordered on genocide.

Three separate scenes of slaughter by the cavalry construct and constitute the motif. The first instance allows the viewer to tolerate the attack by showing only its aftermath: the camera quickly tilts down from an Indian corpse to the saddlebag stamped "US," an allusion to the guilt of our country in this and other attacks on Native peoples. Subsequent massacres become increasingly difficult to bear as the viewer is forced closer to the killing. Jack finds himself in the middle of the second assault, but associated this time with the American soldiers. The editing by Dede Allen fragments the scene, thereby intensifying the commotion and the viewer's identification with Jack's fear, helplessness, and confusion. The third assault, actually carried out by Custer and the Seventh Cavalry in November 1868, takes place at the Washita River. In this long sequence punctuated by graphic violence, the camera, protagonist, victims, and the viewer are together in the very midst of the horror, enclosed by chaos and death, surrounded by fleeing people and falling bodies, screams of terror and cries of pain. Little Big Man escapes the immediate area and watches, powerless to save his wife Sunshine, who, carrying their newborn baby and running desperately, is shot again and again by a ruthless soldier (see fig. 53). The methodical murder of the helpless women and children under Custer's orders may remind an audience of the genocide of Native Americans, that of Jews in the Holocaust, and of the war against the Vietnamese.

The figure and words of Old Lodge Skins unifies the textual connotation of the entire sequence. Characterized as a visionary able to see deeply and clearly even when later blinded, he personifies the noble Indian. In the sequence under study, the camerawork glorifies him in low-angle shots against the sky, his sad gaze and Little Big Man's shocked one in counterpoint with the scene of the slaughter. The camera's framing of the Chief and the weight and tone of his speech contribute to his image as a sage and upright man. He articulates the film's moral theme: the whites lack respect for life, whereas the "Human Beings" (as the Cheyenne refer to themselves) know where the "center of the earth" is and have a profound moral vision of life.

Figure 53. Little Big Man. During the massacre at the Washita River, Sunshine (Amy Eccles) flees from the soldier who shoots her. The viewer shares Little Big Man's point of view as he watches her running toward him.

In the same sequence, Little Big Man appears as a younger reflection of Old Lodge Skins. They wear identical buckskin garments, intricate ornaments, and maroon cloth strips in their braids (see fig. 54). The matching clothing is the symbol of Little Big Man's attainment of his grandfather's wisdom: he has completed his development and is now a full-fledged member of the Cheyenne. One day he will assume his grandfather's place as tribal spokesman by setting the record straight. Jack Crabb's retelling of the Cheyenne's story, taped in the Veterans Administration hospital, preserves the legacy of Old Lodge Skins and his people. The audience accepts the old chief's pronouncements and, therefore, identifies with Jack's growing affinity for the Cheyenne, joining him in his criticism of American colonialism and imperialism.

While this analysis is by no means exhaustive, it demonstrates that the theme and textual motifs of the film are present even in this one brief sequence. The sequence introduces both the first specific presentation of American military aggression and the first formal contrast of Indian moral vision with white moral corruption. The contrast is made by the

Figure 54. Little Big Man. Chief Old Lodge Skins (Chief Dan George) and
Little Big Man (Dustin Hoffman), dressed identically, pause at the site of the
first Indian massacre. "I don't understand it, Grandfather. Why would they kill
women and children?" The old man replies, "Because they are strange."

juxtaposition of the old man's words with the image of the army saddle-bag. The film is clearly critical of the American soldiers; the once-heroic cavalry that could always be counted on to ride to the rescue of belea-guered white settlers has become a band of barbaric, invading butchers, bent on the destruction of an innocent people.

■ Conclusion

Little Big Man, in effect, picks up where John Ford's *Cheyenne Autumn* leaves off. Instead of taking the usual stance of the Hollywood Western —showing white civilization taming the West and bettering the country through progress—it criticizes the frivolity and avarice of "civilization" and accuses it of destroying a benevolent native culture for profit. By invert-ing the conventions of the genre and explicitly demythologizing the westward expansion, the film offers an alternative view of the history of the American West.

Although the film does not provide accurate ethnographic portrayals, it contributes to a more sensitive representation of Native Americans by presenting Old Lodge Skins as a true hero and his culture in a positive light. As the conflict between whites and Indians develops, the movie depicts the cavalry members, not the Indians, as the real savages—bru-tal, corrupt, and insanely violent. Because the Cheyenne are presented as Human Beings, endowed with the best qualities of humankind, the viewer sympathizes with them. Unlike most Hollywood films in which whites play Indians, Arthur Penn cast Native Americans in many major and minor parts, which greatly contributed to the film's authenticity.

Little Big Man is important not only because of its revisionist view of American frontier history and its more sensitive and authentic represen-tation of Native Americans, but also because the film introduces a narrative structure that Westerns of the 1990s subsequently adopted. The story unfolds through the eyes of a white man who, moving and living among Native peoples, gradually becomes disillusioned with his own culture, and, deeply changed by his experiences, casts off his Euro-Ameri-can identity. He learns the ways and language of the natives, dons their garb, accepts an Indian name, and is initiated into the tribal community. The spectator, who identifies with the protagonist, changes along with him and comes to share his appreciation and understanding of the Indians. This initiation archetype relates *Little Big Man* structurally—but not in tone—to *Dances With Wolves* (1990), *Black Robe* (1991), and *The Last of the Mohicans* (1992).

This chapter offers a brief discussion of Pepe Danquart's _Black Rider_ and Arthur Penn's _Little Big Man_ to illustrate the many levels of meaning a film can create, and the ways in which the viewer can approach the text and read those meanings. The same critical methodology can be used to analyze both short and feature-length films.

Chapter 8

The American Industry

Americans mainly see American films. More than 90 percent of the films exhibited and available to viewers in the United States are produced in this country. The major studios release over 400 films annually, but few foreign films find distribution outlets here. In 2001, for instance, 46 foreign-language films were officially submitted for Academy Award consideration; only 8 were picked up by American distributors. These Oscar hopefuls are but a fraction of the motion pictures produced throughout the world. But because of film distribution and marketing practices in the United States, Americans generally see only the Academy Award winner for best foreign film (see fig. 55). These policies boost domestic box-office revenues and, combined with the increasing popularity of American movies abroad, help the American motion picture industry gross over seven billion dollars a year. Like other businesses, the film industry's aim is to maximize profits, so revenues and "entertainment" are more important to executives than "social conscience," "art," or "education."

This book has examined film as a form of expression that combines technical and artistic areas, looking at the means by which films tell stories, create emotions, and convey ideas and information. Its emphasis so far has been on the way movies make meaning and the way viewers read or interpret meaning. At this point some knowledge of film financing, distribution, and exhibition—the market forces that drive production—

Figure 55. Crouching Tiger, Hidden Dragon (d. Ang Lee, 2000). Because of film distribution and marketing practices in the United States, Americans generally see only the Academy Award winner for best foreign-language film. Jen (Zhang Ziyi) showcases her martial arts skills in this crossover hit, which won the Oscar and became the highest grossing foreign film in American box-office history.

can provide fuller understanding of the media. Executives of studios, agencies, distribution companies, theater chains, television stations, and cable companies make decisions that affect the kinds and number of films produced, and, therefore, what viewers see.

In the 1930s and 1940s, the Hollywood studios had enormous economic and social power. Studios could count on box office receipts from a loyal moviegoing public: 65 percent of the American population went to the movies every week. The five largest studios at that time—the "Big Five" —were Warner Brothers, Metro-Goldwyn-Mayer, Paramount, RKO, and Twentieth Century Fox. They owned valuable real estate property in the form of backlots and movie theaters in urban areas all across the country. The studios controlled the entire film process: the producers chose the screenplays and, since they kept directors, writers, actors, and crews under contract, they could put together a production without having to negotiate fees and salaries for each film. Producers planned publicity campaigns to be carried out by staff publicists, decided where and when the films would be shown, and set the rental prices. The studios produced the movies, operated distribution outlets that rented them out, and owned the chains of theaters that played them. This complete control of the film process—from development to exhibition—eliminated competition. **Vertical integration**, as this structure is called, meant that the studios had nearly unlimited artistic and financial control over films. From 1920 to the mid-1940s, with almost complete power over production, distribution, and exhibition, the American film industry grew, unchecked, into a monopoly returning enormous revenues.

The First World War—the years between 1914 and 1918—also contributed to Hollywood's success. Because European countries were fighting, their film industries remained inactive while the American industry was untouched and fully productive. After the war, Europeans were hungry for entertainment. American films were readily available, and because these were silent films, language was no barrier and the works produced could be booked into all foreign countries. The product was in perfect harmony with historical and market forces. This period launched the rise of Hollywood.

Throughout the 1930s, largely because of the Great Depression and the fact that movies were cheap entertainment, the industry remained healthy. Well into the 1940s, it was a central financial power in the entertainment industry. No one could imagine a time when this would no longer be true. But after the Second World War, social, economic, and political changes occurred that had far-reaching effects on American life. Forces revived that had existed in the United States but were kept dormant during the Depression and the war. Four of these forces affected Hollywood directly but differently. Their influence and significance varied somewhat, but their combined effect dismantled the old studio system.

■ Influences on the Hollywood Industry

The Paramount Decrees. This was the name given to a legal attack launched against the studios. In the 1930s, stiff anti-trust laws brought Hollywood's monopolistic practices under government scrutiny. Under the monopoly, theater owners had to agree, before the films were even made, to exhibit an entire block of films produced by a single studio. Usually this group consisted of several desirable titles featuring major stars but also included many more of questionable quality with unknown titles, actors, and subject matter. This all-or-nothing distribution policy, **block-booking**, became the basis of the government's lawsuit against the studios, which argued that such practices fixed prices and restricted competition. World War II delayed the suit, but in 1948, the government won judgment against the studios. The settlement eliminated guaranteed exhibition of studio films, as the studios agreed to divest themselves of their theater chains. This became known as the "consent decrees" or "Paramount decrees," because Paramount was the most powerful of the affected studios. This lawsuit was not the only assault on the monopolistic practices of the industry, but it was the final and most successful effort to break up the three-part system of production, distribution, and exhibition. Although the studios took many years to comply with the Supreme Court order, by the late 1950s, they had sold off many of their theaters: out of the 1,395 theaters giant Paramount owned in 1945, less than a third, or 534, remained in 1957. The smaller RKO owned 109 theaters in 1945 and retained more than half, 82, in 1957. Divestiture increased competition from both American independent and foreign filmmakers and companies, because previously inaccessible theatrical venues were now open to them. For a time, the judgment against the studios effectively limited their economic control and added to Hollywood's growing problems.

Demographics. Another factor was the shift in America's demographics. The postwar baby boom, a large bubble in the population, began in 1946. Along with the novelty of television, the baby boom changed people's habits around entertainment. Families with small children found it less convenient and more expensive to get out for an evening at the movies. Although the Cold War and the Korean War produced more and higher paying jobs, especially in the defense industry, and the wartime shortages of gasoline were over, people were spending their disposable income differently: on children and homes—especially in the suburbs, farther away from movie theaters which were usually located in urban centers. In addition, other kinds of entertainment—live theater, restaurants, concerts, nightclubs—that had been largely unavailable during the Depression and the war were attracting customers. Suddenly the movies, which had been the only form of fun and inexpensive escape for so many years, were only one of many options for the veterans and their families. The number of movie theater admissions fell sharply, another economic blow. The drop in revenues meant a drop in film production.

Television. Coinciding with the postwar emphasis on home and family, television arrived on the scene and has remained a permanent component of Hollywood. In 1947 there were only 14,000 TV sets in America, fewer than one in eight homes, but in 1950, only three years later, there were 4 million, and four years after that, 32 million. In 1962, less than fifteen years after the introduction of TV, it was estimated that 90 percent of all American homes had a set, and people of all ages were spending many hours a week in front of it.

During the early 1950s, and seen as a direct result of the proliferation of TV, attendance at movie theaters fell by 25 percent. TV was stealing the very same audience that had gone faithfully twice a week to the movies for escapist entertainment and had paid regularly to see melodramas, family shows, comedies, thrillers, horror and sci-fi movies, and, of course, Westerns. Television programming was based on these genres—plus old movies, now all available at home "for free." During that period, about one quarter of all movie theaters, 4,000 out of approximately 18,000, closed (although, interestingly, the other great postwar commercial phenomenon, the automobile, contributed to a partial and temporary supplement —the drive-in theater, which for a time became very popular, at least in good weather, accounting for 20 percent of revenues until upkeep became too expensive).

In retrospect, and with nearly a half century of clear-eyed hindsight, Hollywood's response to TV seems fairly predictable: It would do what TV could not do. If the TV screen was small, make the movie screen enormous. If TV was in black and white, make movies "in living color" and with vivid stories in exciting, exotic locations. If TV flattened the image, give movies the illusion of three dimensions. If TV showed only family fare, go after the youth and adult audience. In 1952, when the box office success of Cinerama (a multiple-camera widescreen process) seemed to prove that people would go out to see something that they could not see at home, Hollywood regained hope. The industry thought new technology was the key to success. After Cinerama, 3-D came along with disposable eyeglasses, and then widescreen productions without glasses: Cinemascope, VistaVision, and Todd-AO. The studios occasionally tried gimmicks such as Smell-O-Vision. Today, movie theaters continue to use the wide screen and have incorporated important improvements in sound technology.

Occasionally the movies seemed to make a successful stand against TV. But actually the silver screen could not hold out against the tiny tube; film production costs were so high that good returns on investment were not assured. Rather quickly, the production studios moved to collaborate with the new medium, recognizing that instead of competing, they could profit from a share of TV's many new markets. The studios began by selling old films to TV, then more recent ones, and very soon, big features. Then they began to produce films specifically for TV; and finally they rented out their studio space for TV productions. Eventually the relationship between film and TV became mutually dependent: TV took over the low-end production—Westerns, spy and thriller stories, serials, melodramas or soaps—and left the high-end, more prestigious productions to Hollywood. This division continued until the late 1990s when the cable networks began to produce films specifically for TV.

The Blacklist. The social and political factor that affected big changes in Hollywood was the blacklist. It had its roots in the economic upheavals of the Great Depression in the 1930s. While unemployment mounted in all fields, Hollywood executives were profiting handsomely. Workers began to organize and join labor unions as a way of dealing with what they saw as their exploitation. The Hollywood studios, like other corporations, considered unions a threat to free enterprise. However, in Hollywood, educated people who were working on creative projects believed that world political and social causes were as important as fairness in the local workplace. Many individuals made time and financial commitments to progressive activities and organizations. At the same time, under pressure from the large corporations, Congress established a legislative committee to investigate Communist activities in the United States, which is how labor union activities were always characterized. During the Second World War, the investigations were put on hold because at the time the United States was allied with the Communist Soviet Union against the German Nazis. But immediately after the war, Russia became the enemy, the Cold War began, and the House of Representatives resurrected its Committee on Un-American Activities. This committee investigated progressives in all walks of life, but the hearings on Hollywood attracted the greatest public attention. Then the junior senator from Wisconsin, Joseph McCarthy, taking advantage of the growing climate of suspicion, began his accusations against liberals in the government and gave his name to the entire era: McCarthyism began its rise.

Starting in 1947 and continuing well into the 1950s, the House Committee on Un-American Activities—HUAC—held hearings on the so-called Communist infiltration of Hollywood, claiming that the American public was being influenced by subversive, anti-American political agendas in the movies. To support that claim, the FBI was called in for surveillance of suspected activists. Although HUAC called many film industry workers to testify about their past and current political affiliations, it particularly sought out Hollywood stars. When a HUAC member was mentioned in the newspaper or photographed with John Wayne, Humphrey Bogart, or Gary Cooper, enormous publicity was generated which lent credibility and a certain legitimacy to the Committee itself. Hollywood executives, fearing government intervention, hastened to announce that they would "cleanse" the studios of the "Communist threat." They stated publicly that they would not hire Communists or fellow travelers, as Communist sympathizers were termed. Quietly, a blacklist was created: an actual list of people who were accused of Communist affiliation or sympathy. Only some of the people were or had been members of the Communist Party, but many had worked for progressive or radical causes like the Spanish Civil War relief. All were deprived of their jobs and found themselves unemployable. What made the blacklist most deplorable was that neither the American Communist Party (CPUSA) itself nor membership in it was at any time illegal in the United States. It was difficult to find a legal basis on which to fight the defamation, yet people's lives were destroyed by the mere association of their name with Communism, and any progressive association was called Communism.

Looking back, the hearings clearly were damaging not only to those individuals who were fired from their jobs but to the whole film community. People were called as witnesses before HUAC and asked to give the names of colleagues, friends, and acquaintances who they knew or suspected were members of the Communist Party. The witnesses found themselves confronted with an ethical dilemma. A few courageous or already-famous individuals, such as Lillian Hellman and Humphrey Bogart, refused to provide names (although Bogart subsequently retracted his strong stand against the Committee). Others pleaded to be excused from testifying, wishing to be saved from becoming stool-pigeons. Still others took the First Amendment, which guarantees freedom of speech, or the Fifth, which preserves a person from testifying against him or herself. They all found themselves blacklisted because they had been "unfriendly" witnesses or because "taking the Fifth" came to imply guilt. The "friendly" witnesses named others, often without proof and sometimes only because they disliked the person. Without a trial, since they broke no law, without the opportunity to answer or disprove the charges, without the support of or resistance by studio executives, those named were immediately barred from working in Hollywood and, eventually, in television. A group of men who became known as the Hollywood Ten went to prison, not for being members of the Communist Party but for contempt of Congress, because they stood up for free speech, citing the First Amendment, and refused to testify about their own or other people's political activities and beliefs.

Between 1950 and 1960, the blacklist contained the names of two or three hundred people (although suspicion was so widespread that much higher figures were presumed). Larry Ceplair and Steven Englund explain in their book, *The Inquisition in Hollywood*, how the blacklist eventually unraveled. First, in 1959, the blacklisted writer Nedrick Young announced that he had written the Academy Award-winning script of *The Defiant Ones* (1957) under an assumed name. A short time later, the once preeminent writer Dalton Trumbo stated that he was "Robert Rich" who had won an Academy Award for the script of *The Brave One*, back in 1956. Trumbo, one of the Hollywood Ten, had been jailed, released, and blacklisted, and had for years been writing under assumed names using a "front" to sell his scripts. Then, in 1960, Otto Preminger announced that Trumbo had written *Exodus* in 1959, and that he would be given screen credit upon the film's imminent release. Preminger's courageous action inspired Kirk Douglas and Universal Pictures to credit Trumbo onscreen as the writer of *Spartacus*, which they were about to release. These steps contributed to the blacklist's slow collapse.

The blacklist had great impact on Hollywood. Most obviously, some very talented individuals were denied work, left the industry or the United States, and took their skills and creative ideas with them. For another thing, it deeply divided the film community into those who saw the "friendly witnesses" as either informers or patriots and the resistors as either heroes or traitors. Even after their return from prison the Hollywood Ten continued to suffer, as their punishment did not end with serving their prison sentences; they could not work because no one would hire them. Other blacklistees were openly kept under surveillance by the FBI. These experiences, along with the idea that jobs could be lost because of a rumor or personal antipathy, caused such general fear and insecurity that a shift occurred in the kinds of movies that the industry dared to make. Writers were afraid to write; producers were afraid to produce; directors were afraid of being associated with a questionable film. The content of films had to exclude portrayals of poverty, workers, minorities, any socially conscious subject material that had begun to trickle into the movies of the 1930s and wartime. Now once again, films treated issues around women, war, crime, and social problems in a predictable and unquestioning way if at all. Innovations and novel ideas in subject matter or form which might have benefited Hollywood in the new competitive climate were not even put forward because they were risky. If the resulting film was too socially conscious, it might be misunderstood, seen as subversive or leftist, or just dangerously different; newly independent theater owners might refuse to book it into their theaters. All these circumstances contributed to a definite chilling effect on film production as the industry continued to perfect its mixture of tame, dilute subject matter (love stories, comedies, adventures) and safe, simple forms (musicals, historical costume dramas, extravaganzas). Whenever the box office gross dipped, which it did throughout the decade, Hollywood, seeking the winning formula and with only the most rudimentary notion of a targeted audience, clutched at whatever seemed to attract audiences: more extravagant musicals, more terrifying horror films, youth culture and sexploitation films.

The consequences of the blacklist were felt by individuals in their personal lives and relationships. Friendships, families, and marriages were hurt and sometimes destroyed. The ideological split in the once close-knit movie industry generated rage and bitterness, but perhaps the greatest damage was to the United States Constitution, the Bill of Rights, and freedom of speech, freedom of belief, and the right to remain silent.

In 1972 Martin Ritt, who had been blacklisted, made a comedy about a blacklisted writer who found a friend to sell his work. *The Front* was written by Walter Bernstein, also blacklisted, and featured several actors and actresses who had been blacklisted. Not only were they given screen credit at the end of the film, but the dates during which they were deprived of work were noted as well. In 1991 Irwin Winkler made *Guilty By Suspicion* with Robert De Niro as a blacklisted director. The film seriously explores the way Hollywood hounded and persecuted its own. In 1997, on the fiftieth anniversary of the first HUAC hearings, thanks to the tireless work of Paul Jarrico, blacklisted writers' names were finally restored to the screen credits of the films they wrote during "the plague years."

Dealing with these factors was very troublesome for Hollywood which, until the early 1950s, had not needed to consider either demographics or competition. In any case, the industry could do little about the baby boom except wait for the children to grow up and become moviegoers themselves. All it did about the blacklist was wait until the political climate in America gradually changed in the 1960s and HUAC lost its power. Hollywood's relationship with TV permanently affected both industries. As for vertical integration, it is alive and well in the current industry, corporate monopolistic practices having been legalized during the presidency of Ronald Reagan.

■ Current Circumstances

Hollywood set box-office records in 2000 with revenues of $7.5 billion in the domestic market alone. For the second year in a row, declining admissions were offset by a rise in ticket prices. The big surprise was the $20 billion income generated by the video market: $11.6 billion in videotape and DVD sales and $8.3 billion in rentals. Although only two films passed the $200 million mark at the box office, Disney's top three video titles made more than $200 million apiece. While the top five film releases brought in $900 million, the top five videos passed the $1.17 billion mark. The staggering video numbers were largely due to a 269 percent increase in DVD sales and rentals from the previous year, making the DVD format the fastest-growing, most widely accepted new technology in home entertainment. So for the first time in motion picture history, the video market outperformed theatrical releases—by nearly triple the take.

Because over 400 films are released in the United States each year, at least one major film opens every weekend, giving moviegoers a large number of choices and helping to establish their moviegoing habit. At the same time, star salaries have soared to $20 million or more per movie and special effects-driven films have inflated production costs as high as $200 million. Today the average cost to make and market a single feature is more than $82 million, about $55 million for production expenses and $27 million for prints and advertising. Most studios release at least one expensive "event movie" per season and a blockbuster every week during the summer. Despite rising costs, the studios have remained profitable due to their aftermarket customers: pay-per-view, pay channel and basic cable; network television; home video; and overseas markets.

During the take-over frenzy of the 1980s and early 1990s, the seven major Hollywood studios were absorbed by huge conglomerates. Warner Communications merged with Time, Inc. to form Time Warner, Inc.—the world's largest communications conglomerate—and subsequently acquired Turner Broadcasting and Fine Line Features. Gulf and Western Industries (or Engulf and Devour, as Mel Brooks called it in *Silent Movie*) became Paramount Communications, Inc. whose media holdings include Paramount Pictures, broadcast stations, and cable systems; then Paramount merged with Viacom/CBS to become one of the world's leading producers of filmed entertainment and cable programming. Twentieth Century Fox was bought by Australian communications magnate Rupert Murdoch, becoming part of his News Corporation. Columbia merged with distributor/producer TriStar to become Columbia Pictures Entertainment and then signed a merger agreement with Japan's Sony Corporation and was renamed Sony Pictures Entertainment. Ted Turner resold MGM/UA to Kirk Kerkorian, who sold it to Pathé Communications before it was taken over by the French bank, Credit Lyonnais, and then sold to an investment group managed by Kerkorian; the name has been restored to Metro-Goldwyn-Mayer, Inc., but the studio only operates on a limited basis.

Meanwhile, Disney has become a major player. In addition to its Disney, Touchstone Pictures, Hollywood Pictures, and Buena Vista divisions, the company acquired Miramax, the leading independent producer/distributor, and ABC. The company is heavily invested in the Disney theme parks and retail stores worldwide, self-sustaining enterprises that also function as publicity mechanisms for the company's movies. MCA, the parent company of Universal Pictures, was bought by Japan's Matsushita Electric Industrial Company, Ltd. in 1990, becoming part of the world's most diversified entertainment conglomerate; five years later, the Seagram Co. acquired MCA and then sold it to Vivendi, a French-controlled conglomerate. DreamWorks SKG—founded by Steven Spielberg, Jeffrey Katzenberg, and David Geffen—was the first major studio to open in fifty years, having released its first feature in 1997, and remains the only privately held studio. With the exception of MGM and DreamWorks, all these companies form media organizations so thoroughly integrated that the old studios could hardly have dreamed of such monopoly and the possibility for cross-promotion over so many communication outlets.

Recently giants Time Warner and America Online merged in the nation's biggest media marriage, positioning the new company to lead the future convergence of television, high-speed connections, and the Web. This new model may some day allow American Online users to download an extensive library of Time Warner movies, music, and magazines on high-speed cable lines—as well as connect users to e-commerce, interactive television, and message services. In the last two decades, the industry has radically restructured itself vertically and globally.

Despite megamergers and innovative technology, the escalating costs and risks associated with big-budget filmmaking encourage studio partnerships in a "split-rights" world. Universal and Sony joined forces for _Erin Brockovich_, with the former taking the domestic rights. Universal took the foreign rights when partnering with DreamWorks for _Gladiator_. When the budget for _Almost Famous_ reached $80 million, DreamWorks worked out a co-financing arrangement with Sony. The financing and rights to _Crouching Tiger, Hidden Dragon_ was split among four companies.

Many changes have occurred among the independents, most of which began as distribution companies. Established "indies" such as Miramax, Fine Line, TriStar, October Films, and Polygram Films have been absorbed by major studios and now are considered their specialty divisions. Other production companies, including Clint Eastwood's Malpaso and Spike Lee's Forty Acres and a Mule, have long-time affiliations with the majors for financing and distribution. The smaller indies work out their own financing arrangements, make their own films, and self-distribute or have their films picked up for distribution. Such independent production/distribution companies as the Shooting Gallery and Revolution Studios have a relatively small output, releasing fewer than twelve features a year.

■ Production

Power is no longer concentrated in the studios, nor do studio heads control the film industry as they did during Hollywood's Golden Age. Today studio executives are hired hands; they do not own the studios as did the moguls in the 1930s and 1940s, so they can be fired by a corporate studio's board of directors. Real power today often rests in the hands of producers and agents (see fig. 56). **Producers** are the deal makers, the ones who develop projects and must obtain a substantial amount of financing to get a film in production. Today's producers tend to view the studios as distribution entities that provide the leverage to attract outside investors. In charge of the business of making a film, producers assume responsibility for a movie's commercial success or failure. They bring in writers to make script revisions and hire and fire directors. They can pressure directors to speed up production or bring down costs. They can demand final cut, having the final say on how a film should be edited for release, and they accept the Oscars for Best Picture during the Academy Awards.

Agents often package the deals because they represent a roster of many types of talent. During the studio years, all the actors, screenwriters, and

Figure 56. Cartoonist Nicole Hollander comments on the scant supply of meaningful roles for women in the movies. From *I'm In Training to Be Tall and Blonde.* © 1979 by Nicole Hollander. Reprinted by permission of the artist.

directors were under contract. Today these people are free to select firms such as Creative Artists Agency to negotiate their assignments and contracts. Agents, therefore, control access to talent. An agent can attach a top director and a star to a script written by another client; then the agent can present the package to various studios in hopes of completing the deal.

Directors with strong track records can command artistic control of a project from inception to completion. Some of them function as producer-directors—George Lucas, Francis Coppola, Steven Spielberg—by establishing their own production companies, and thereby control and reap maximum profits from their projects. But they must find a distributor. New talent is emerging from every media, with MTV opening most doors for newcomers such as McG (*Charlie's Angels*) and Robert Luketic (*Legally Blonde*). Directors are also crossing over from television series, advertising, theater, comics, documentaries, video games, acting, and television animation. Film schools no longer provide the main road to industry jobs.

Some independent filmmakers have become well-known and relatively successful ***auteurs***, artists who express a personal vision throughout their

Figure 57. *Passion Fish* (d. John Sayles, 1992). Independent filmmaker John Sayles has become a well-known and relatively successful auteur. David Strathairn, Alfre Woodard, and Mary McDonnell star in this unique drama noted for its strong women's roles, honest handling of such sensitive issues as disability and interracial friendship, and evocative rendering of the Cajun culture.

(Photograph by Bob Marshak, ©1992)

Figure 58. Do the Right Thing (d. Spike Lee, 1990). In 1986 Spike Lee directed a very low-budget film, *She's Gotta Have It,* which was so successful that it launched his career and enabled him to write, direct, and star in this film with Danny Aiello.

(Copyright © by Universal City Studios, Inc. Courtesy of MCA Publishing Rights, a Division of MCA Inc.)

body of work. For example, since 1980, John Sayles has written, directed, and produced MORE than a dozen films including *The Brother From Another Planet, Matewan, City of Hope, Passion Fish* (see fig. 57), and *Lone Star*. Spike Lee's first feature was a very low-budget film, *She's Gotta Have It,* which did so well that it launched his career and enabled him to make SUCH films AS *Do the Right Thing* (see fig. 58) and *Malcolm X.* Jim

Jarmusch's story is quite similar: his second film, *Stranger Than Paradise*, was made inexpensively and received good reviews that led to its national distribution. That success allowed him to make *Down By Law, Mystery Train, Night on Earth,* and others. Darren Aronofsky became a Sundance favorite with *Pi* and won much acclaim for his stylishly directed *Requiem For A Dream.* All of these productions have played to a small but interested following. These independent films have an "individual stamp" and stand as alternatives to Hollywood products, which often are formulaic and seem to have been made by committee.

Recently independent film has become a hot topic and a difficult term to define. From the mid-1940s through the early 1970s, artists such as Maya Deren and Stan Brakhage, using amateur 8mm and 16mm formats produced avant-garde work that challenged accepted notions of film language and aesthetics. They were committed to presenting alternative points of view rather than generating profits. When John Sayles and a handful of mavericks started working outside the studio mainstream in the late 1970s, their independent works starred unknown actors and were defiantly edgier and definitely less expensive than studio films. These films won critical and commercial acclaim in the early 1980s, obtained distribution in first-run theaters, and challenged the Hollywood product.

The explosive success of independent features, from Steven Soderbergh's *sex, lies and videotape* through Quentin Tarantino's *Pulp Fiction,* convinced the studios to buy existing independent companies or start their own. At the same time, many first-time filmmakers hoped to become the next rags-to-riches story or to gain entry into the Hollywood mainstream through independent productions. As a result of these two factors, the line has blurred between studio and independent films. Instead of trying to break away from a standard Hollywood model, independent films end up for the most part embracing it. Now they tend to be more expensive productions, catering to more traditional tastes and featuring top stars. But even celebrated producers, writers, directors, and stars cannot get controversial projects funded. Saul Zaentz, who had won Best Picture Oscars for *One Flew Over the Cuckoo's Nest* and *Amadeus,* could not convince Twentieth Century Fox to produce *The English Patient;* the studio felt Ralph Fiennes and Juliette Binoche were not big enough stars (subsequently the film won nine Academy Awards, including best supporting actress for Binoche). Robert Duvall financed *The Apostle* (1997) with $5 million of his own money after the studios and independent production companies refused to support the film (see fig. 59), feeling its religious subject matter was not commercially viable. Because of this situation, the corporate studios continue to retain power, and independent-spirited filmmakers struggle to produce vital and challenging material.

Almost all documentary films are independently produced because of their minuscule commercial value. Fundraising for these projects is most

Figure 59. The Apostle (d. Robert Duvall, 1997). Writer/director/star Robert Duvall financed this film with $5 million of his own money, because the studios were not willing to risk investment on religious subject matter.

difficult: documentary filmmakers apply to government funding agencies, corporate foundations, and private sponsors. Occasionally funding is provided by television: the Corporation for Public Broadcasting supports documentaries, which are then shown on PBS, and cable television stations such as HBO and TNT fund programs and films for broadcast on their stations.

■ Distribution

Traditionally distributors are the link between the producer and the exhibitor. The industry has changed so radically in such a short period of time that separating the functions of distribution and exhibition has become more difficult. Companies are consolidating to perform these functions which seem entirely based on finances, legalities, and competition.

Technically the goal of the **distributor** is to position a film in theaters and regions of the country where it can best reach its target audience. For theatrical releases, the distributor begins to publicize the film by sending out advance press releases on the stars, the location, the costs, and on any problems of production that may have occurred. These preliminary notices get the film "into the public mind" and create anticipation. Once the film is completed, it is test-marketed. Everything from preview screenings to telephone surveys are used and, depending on the response, the film's ending might be changed and an entire advertising campaign organized. Print coverage in the daily press and in major magazines involves a range of more detailed information on the production of the film. Trailers are previews that run in movie theaters, on television, on the Internet, and on video releases to advertise a film. Big advertising campaigns contribute to big box office. And big box office contributes to higher video sales.

Distributors have begun to use the Internet to market movies, considering a dedicated Web site an inexpensive way to raise the odds that a movie will make money. Sometimes they mount elaborate marketing campaigns that try to involve moviegoers before the film hits the theaters. *The Blair Witch Project* site, which craftily mixed reality and myth, drew a huge following whose word-of-mouth fueled the film's success in 1999.

Although production stills and interviews are conventional features on such Web sites, inventive online promotional campaigns create the most buzz. An enormous interactive Web game, involving about thirty sites dedicated to solving the mysterious murder of Evan Chan, promoted Steven Spielberg's *A.I. Artificial Intelligence.* Puzzles and clues popped up everywhere. At an appearance to discuss the movie, a presumably planted audience member at the Massachusetts Institute of Technology asked star

Haley Joel Osment what it was like to work with Jeanine Salla, who is credited in the film as "sentient machine therapist." She does not exist, but she did have her own Web site. Several sites promoted the freedom campaign of the artificial intelligence robots, and one site even had a working phone number.

Some Web sites encourage gameplaying, share privileged information, or reveal behind-the-scenes activity. Twentieth Century Fox stashed collectible props from *Planet of the Apes* in locations around the world and, working with Geocaching.com, announced the coordinates. The studio was the first to use Global Positioning Technology (GPS) and scavenger sport as a marketing tool. A 3-D surround camera chronicled the making of *Lord of the Rings* and uploaded the footage more than a year before the film's release. Such "viral marketing"—spreading like an Internet virus —gains influence and market share among small, focused audiences.

New technology also enables filmmakers to challenge established distribution channels. Short films have benefited most from Internet exposure. Once confined to festival showings, they have found a wider audience through sites devoted exclusively to them, such as AtomFilms.com and IFILM.com. Joe Nussbaum's *George Lucas in Love*, a clever nine-minute spoof of *Star Wars* and *Shakespeare in Love*, became an instant Internet hit on MediaTrip.com and then a top seller when released exclusively on video by Amazon.com. After watching the music industry fumble through the Internet revolution, Sony Pictures Digital Entertainment and Warner Bros. have made arrangements to sell movie downloads through a service called Movielink, an Internet movie-on-demand service. Disney and Viacom Entertainment Group have their own venture, Movies.com. The spread of high-speed Internet access will spur more Internet film viewing and downloaded rental copies of feature films.

Marketing is carefully calculated and based on a decision about the release pattern, the number and location of the theaters into which a film will be released. Distributors decide on whether the film will open wide or limited. As the name implies, wide release is the distribution of a film to many theaters all at the same time. This "front-loading" strategy is used for big-budget movies designed as blockbusters (*Spider-Man* opened on 8,000 screens), and also for those films whose reception is predicted to be poor. Wide release costs a great deal because several thousand prints must be struck and shipped along with advertising packages to the theaters. The object is to orchestrate a record-breaking debut, sell the film based on the names of the stars and director, and build audience expectation. This approach is not always successful, but films can gain attention by reporting good opening-week performance, which helps garner more money in the video, television, and foreign ancillary markets.

Limited release is employed for smaller films on which executives decide not to risk expenditures on prints and advertising. Limited release films usually open in cities in which demographics suggest a receptive audience; they appear in selected theaters in hopes of attracting an audience through local appeal, good reviews, or word of mouth. Independent productions usually open in limited release, if only because they rarely have access to large distribution outlets.

Deserving independent films do not always get picked up by a distributor. Rob Nilsson's *Heat and Sunlight* won the grand prize at the U.S. Film Festival in 1988 and received rave reviews from critics around the world. Yet distributors in this country were reluctant to release it, so Nilsson and his colleagues assumed the arduous task of self-distribution that allowed the film to reach audiences on a limited basis. When Zeitgeist Films decided not to distribute the Spanish-language *La Ciudad*, a narrative film about new immigrants, director David Riker convinced Latin American theater owners in New York City to give him a cash advance. He bought three prints of his film and advertising, and released the movie in the city's Latino theaters where it outperformed Hollywood blockbusters for six weeks in 1999. For every movie like *Shine*, which was acquired at the Sundance Film Festival, many more films never find a distributor.

Recently the marketplace has polarized, favoring blockbusters launched with marketing blitzes or small specialized releases that need delicate handling. Without a star, the likelihood of getting any type of financing from domestic or foreign distribution sources is slim. Name casting drives consumer interest, so the catch phrase "Get a star on your side" serves as good advice.

Distributors approach the international market as separate sections of the world, each with its own customs, advertising psychology, and seasons. Although some films are released simultaneously in the United States and overseas, a number of factors dictate release dates abroad: marketing and promotional considerations, local competition, and availability of touring talent.

■ Exhibition

Another area that has changed greatly is exhibition. Due to increasingly fierce competition and the precarious status of exhibitors, exhibition practices seem to change almost daily. The population shift to the suburbs resulted in an increase in the number of shopping-mall movie theaters. Some of these are owned by the corporations that also own the studios; others are owned by independent theater chains. In both cases the exhibitors need to produce profits, so they want successful movies, blockbusters if possible, that will keep a steady stream of customers coming into the theaters for weeks (the newspapers provide free publicity by publishing the weekly "score" on the top-grossing films). Exhibitors used to bid on a film based entirely on the studio's advance publicity, gambling on the film's box-office success. These days gross percentages have replaced up-front fees. Theater owners do not disclose how much they pay distributors for movie rentals, but the number is believed to be 50 to 55 percent of the ticket price. Film splits heavily favor the distributors in the first few weeks of a movie's release but subsequently favor theater operators.

Exhibitors never know which releases will do well at the box office. Kevin Costner's *Dances With Wolves* seemed destined to fail because it was a western with subtitles and a running time of more than three hours. However, the film was a surprising success and was among the top-grossing films of 1991. In contrast, Costner's *The Postman* was the biggest flop of 1997, while *Bean* and *The Full Monty*, minor foreign releases that year, surprised the industry when they became big hits. The computer-animated *Shrek* was the smash of the 2001 summer season, not the heavily promoted *Pearl Harbor* or *Planet of the Apes*. With many films crowding the marketplace, first-run houses have adopted an all-or-nothing approach: films that open poorly may be pulled in their first days of release and never have a chance to find an audience.

With few exceptions, the old single-screen theaters and the smaller repertory theaters and art houses in urban areas are either closing, selling to the chains, or being converted into multiple-screen theaters. In the 1980s, companies were building multiplexes in shopping malls in all areas of rapid population growth, especially in the southern United States. These theaters generated enormous cash flow and could break even when a mere 20 percent of their seats filled. The trend continued in the 1990s with the rise of 20-to-30-screen megaplexes, where exhibitors offer a wide range of films under one roof, often at the same show times, and provide stadium seating, movable armrests, digital sound and lavish concession stands.

Another trend is toward fewer and larger chains. Bigger chains have more power to cut operating costs by combining overhead and getting greater volume discounts on concessions and equipment. Moreover they can negotiate more favorable terms to license films, which leads to bigger profits. But rapid expansion, which was often built on debt, has forced many of the largest chains to file for bankruptcy. The burgeoning supply of theater seats far outstripped attendance, creating financial problems for the industry. According to the National Association of Theatre Owners, between 1994 and 1999, the number of movie screens in the United States grew by 39 percent, but the number of tickets sold grew only 13 percent. The megaplexes built by the chains pulled ticket buyers away from their older theaters, which began to perform poorly. Instead of closing their unprofitable locations, the owners kept them open to defend their territories. Now these chains are restructuring and downsizing.

At a time when the North American cinema business has reached saturation due to overbuilding, Europe looks particularly attractive to Hollywood. The European movie market has expanded steadily since the early 1990s and is set for robust future growth. A multiplex boom has also started in Japan and China. Everyone knows that the real growth for the American film industry will come from the international markets.

Most people in the film industry think a conversion to digital projection will take place. The major studios spend an average of $800 million per year making film prints, an expense that would disappear once the majority of theaters switch from projecting celluloid to all-digital files sent via recorded disc or over a network-based delivery system. Theater owners would be able to juggle films with the click of a mouse: a screen used for a children's film by day could be swapped for an added showing of a sold-out, R-rated hit by night—and the soundtrack could be switched to Spanish in the process. Digital movies, exact duplicates of the studio original, will never get scratched, dirty, or faded. A digital feed could also help theaters draw a premium-paying audience for live sporting events or rock concerts shown on the big screen with state-of-the-art definition and sound. But the massive hardware overhaul would cost an estimated $150,000 for each screen, and many film directors, cinematographers, and spectators remain devoted to celluloid images.

VHS and DVD formats have had a truly staggering impact on exhibition, opening vast new video markets that have grown at an amazing rate. More than 81 percent of American households own videocassette recorders, and an estimated 15 million have DVD players. DVDs will probably become the industry standard because of their superior image quality and massive storage capacity that allows for hours of supplemental information on one small disc. Users have the flexibility to make menu choices at will, choosing among behind-the-scenes documentaries, audio commentaries from filmmakers and critics, and collections of deleted scenes. Such interactivity is changing the way people watch films.

Viewing a film on a television screen or computer monitor does change the experience: the image is flattened, detail is lost, image size is not only smaller but often in a different aspect ratio, edges are rounded rather than sharp, color is modified and modifiable, just to list a few differences. But the success of home viewing testifies to the appeal of individual control over the situation. The low cost appeals to consumers, as well as the idea of choice—the film, hour, level of sound, even food and drink, all are at the viewer's finger tips. For all the negative aesthetic modifications, there are quite a number of attractions.

Significant changes have taken place in the motion picture industry. The old studio system has been absorbed by huge communications conglomerates that are integrated vertically, horizontally, and globally. This handful of corporate giants controls most mainstream media. On the other

Figure 60. Explorers (d. Joe Dante, 1985). An alien tentatively peeks at one of the explorers who arrived in a faraway world of film and television buffs. Later the creature proclaims, "We know what you do to our kind down there." Bennett (Ethan Hawke) replies, "But that's the movies! That's not the way we really are."

hand, the digital revolution has democratized the production process by making affordable digital cameras and editing systems available to anyone who wants to make a movie, and the Internet offers new distribution outlets apart from the traditional Hollywood gatekeepers. Drastic changes in theatrical exhibition may occur in the next ten years. Despite these major transitions, the basic three-part structure of the American film industry remains the same: the producer makes the film, the distributor arranges for its circulation, and the exhibitor shows it in the theater. The players remain the same, even though the game has changed.

■ ■ ■

The films produced in the American industry convey an array of subject matter as well as our culture and values. Some of these are covert and emerge only through analysis and interpretation. Some are overt and fully self-aware. Hollywood never seems to tire of looking at itself. At the end of Joe Dante's *Explorers* (1985), the three boys reach a dwelling in outer space and see that the creatures there have access to all the films and television shows of the last several decades, as they have been broadcast into space (see fig. 60). And what is the result? The extra-terrestrials turn out to be film and TV buffs, avid consumers of the abundant material available on the tube. They speak fluent English, but it is language completely based on television commercials and programs. The "guy" alien perfectly imitates lines from ads and rattles off flawless imitations of movie and television figures; he "does" Ed Sullivan, Groucho Marx, Little Richard, W.C. Fields, and many TV comedians.

Hearing canned lines (and canned laughter), one of the boys, Bennett (Ethan Hawke), worries that "it doesn't make sense." His companion (River Phoenix) explains, "That's the way they think we talk," while behind them TV clips play indiscriminately on a wall-sized screen — Tom and Jerry cartoons, news programs, advertisements, the Paramount logo, *I Love Lucy*, Bob Hope, *The Beverly Hillbillies*, and other material.

The "girl" alien says, "Anyway, we know what you do to our kind down there," and switches the channel to show clips of 1950s sci-fi movies, including *The Day the Earth Stood Still*, *Godzilla*, and *Flying Saucers From Mars*, in all of which the alien creatures are shot, blown up, or attacked.

"But that's only the movies!" cries Bennett, "That's not the way we really are."

Figure 61. *Casablanca.* This film has become an American cultural icon.

The "guy" says to him in his comedian's voice, "You expect me to believe that?" And then he gets more serious: "Your people just like to blow things up."

Bennett tries to explain that "We don't really kill people . . . well, we do . . . but not aliens, because we haven't met any."

The "guy" makes a plea for understanding, friendship, and tolerance. He says that he knows he looks weird to the boys but that they look as weird to him and goes on to say, "I watched four episodes of *Lassie*, before I figured out why the little hairy kid never spoke."

At the end of the film, when the earthlings are leaving, the "girl" gives Bennett a gem, and he asks what it is. The "guy" alien answers in a perfect impersonation of Bogart in *The Maltese Falcon*: "It's the stuff dreams are made of."

"She" then says in Ingrid Bergman's accent from *Casablanca*: "We'll always have Paris."

Ironically, the boys, already space-travelers in the film story, are also "time-travelers" as are we. After all, we and they recognize the allusions and know the material mostly from the same source as the aliens: TV.

So . . . along with rock-and-roll, Groucho Marx, cartoons, ads, old television series, and old science fiction films, the movies have become emblems of our culture (see fig. 61). Countless films are collected, recorded, and beamed into outer space—or at least into other countries in which people think we talk that way and think we live the way depicted on television and the movies. What is the message? Movies and television transmit our culture, our styles, and our values. We should be prepared to understand and interpret what we are seeing and telling others.

Afterword
A Critical Eye

I had called on my friend Sherlock Holmes upon the morning after Christmas to wish him the compliments of the season. "I should like, Watson, to go very soon," said Holmes as we sat down to a cup of holiday cheer. "Go! Where to?" "To the Odeon Cinema," said he.

I was not surprised. Indeed my only wonder was that he had not already invited me to accompany him on his excursions to examine this newest art, which was the single topic of interest across the length and breadth of several counties. "I should be most happy to accompany you if I should not be in the way," said I. "My dear Watson. You would confer a great favor upon me by joining me. And, from my recent experience, I think that your time will not be mis-spent, for there are points about this new invention which promise to have some bearing on the method I have endeavored to establish. That is, to read from the indications presented, the meaning of the visual evidence."

And so it happened that an hour or so later, I found myself at the Odeon, in the seventh row on the aisle. Holmes, his sharp, eager countenance outlined in the half-light, was seated at my side. As the lights continued to dim even further, the music rose, and I felt rather than saw him settle into his chair, his eyes hooded but alert . . . .

"Do you see, Watson?" Holmes whispered during a momentary lull, "The gambler wearing the black leather gloves is the villain and has committed the murder; the other, wearing the white hat and scarf, is the hero and will discover the culprit." "But Holmes," I protested, "how can you possibly know that?" "Elementary, my dear Watson. Evil and good, you know. To decipher the codes, one must have a critical eye. It is of the utmost importance."

Glossary

A

Aerial perspective. Also called atmospheric perspective. Closer objects are in greater detail than distant ones which are in soft tones with blurred outlines.

Allusion. A mention or indirect reference to a person, place, or event external to the work in which it appears. Extending the level of meaning beyond the film itself, an allusion may refer to a literary work, a piece of art, a film, a song, or a cultural issue.

Ambient sound. Sound not connected to specific visible sources but necessary to the creation of a believable setting.

American shot. Fuller than a medium shot, *Plan américain* (named by the French) captures the human figure from mid-calf.

Angle. The position of the camera in relation to the subject.

Angle/reverse angle shot or Shot/reverse shot. The first shot is followed by another taken from the angle opposite to it. Hollywood studios used this shot sequence extensively in the 1930s and 1940s to record conversations between two people.

Art director. Also called the production designer. Researches decor and settings; oversees artists, craftspersons, and decorators for the creation of a set.

Aspect ratio. The ratio of the width to the height of the image.

B

Backlight. The light placed behind a subject to separate it from the background.

Bird's-eye shot. The camera is placed directly overhead, perched "like a bird" looking straight down at the scene. Busby Berkeley used this viewpoint to transform the dancers in his lavish production numbers into kaleidoscopic graphic patterns.

Blocking. Also called choreography. The plotting out of interaction between the movements of the camera and actors to ensure that all are at the right place at the right time, in focus and correctly lit.

Blue-screen photography. The chemical response of certain film stocks to blue light makes it possible to film a figure against a blue screen and then superimpose the image on another background without the blue screen showing.

C

CGI or CG. Computer-generated images.

Cinematographer. Also called the Director of Photography or D.P. In charge of the camera and lighting, she or he selects the exposure, framing, and the setups for each shot according to the director's plan.

Close-up. The camera records an area in which the subject fills the screen with very little background showing. Because this shot reveals a character's feelings, responses, and emotions, the spectator feels an intimacy and involvement with the character.

Color design. The Production Designer works with the Director of Photography and Costume Designer to ensure that the set, lighting, and costuming conform to the director's vision of the film's color design. Bright hues such as red, yellow, and orange tend to attract the spectator's attention, so unless color is controlled, it may disturb the meaning of the shot by making dramatically insignificant characters or objects stand out.

Composite. Combining two or more images through optical or digital processes so they appear to have been photographed at the same time.

Composition. The arrangement of visual elements in the shot. Like painters and other visual artists, filmmakers use design principles to emphasize harmony or chaos within the film frame and to establish a relationship among all the elements of the *mise en scène*.

Continuity. The progression of the narrative, usually based on the logic of the action. Also refers to continuity editing, which permits the spectator to "read" a film without any conscious effort because such editing conventions as match on action and eyeline matches render the cuts invisible. The continuity system creates a smooth flow from shot to shot so that the viewer's attention will not be distracted from the story.

Continuity assistant or script supervisor. The person responsible for ensuring visual consistency from shot to shot and sequence to sequence. Finding continuity errors is one of the ancillary sports of moviegoing today.

Contrast ratio. The proportion between darker and lighter parts of a set or location.

Counterpoint or contrapuntal sound. Music and sound effects in contrast to the image.

Crane shot. A shot taken from a camera mounted on a mechanical device that moves freely along a vertical axis. The crane has a telescoping arm on which the camera operator sits.

Crosscut. The shots alternate between actions occurring in at least two different locations. The editing suggests simultaneity and eventual convergence of the actions, while creating suspense.

Cultural connotation. Understanding based on the things everyone learns about society; ways of living and behaving in a social group; values, assumptions, and expectations.

D

Deep-focus shot. Requires a wide-angle lens and provides maximum depth of field. By allowing the objects in the foreground, middleground, and background planes to remain in sharp focus at the same time, this shot approximates what the human eye can see in the real world and may create significant juxtapositions among people and objects in the various planes. The deep-focus shot, multiplane composition, eye-level camera angle, long take, and continuity editing are important components of the aesthetics of Realist Theory.

Depth of field. The scope of the image in sharp focus.

Dialogue. Lines spoken in conversation between two or more characters.

Digital image processing. Computer-generated images (CGI or CG).

Director. The person in charge of all artistic aspects of a film production: acting, set design, cinematography, sound, and editing (if the contract specifies final cut).

Dissolve. A fade-out superimposed over a fade-in so that one image begins to disappear as the other begins to appear.

Distributor. The company that markets the film and arranges for theatrical exhibition, TV broadcast, or release on videocassette, laserdisc, or DVD.

Dolly shot. The camera films while mounted on a dolly, a miniature crane equipped with wheels. Also known as a tracking or trucking shot.

Dynamic composition. The changing relationship of a number of graphic elements in motion.

E

Editing. The process of arranging and assembling film or video—image and sound—into a specific order to convey meaning. Editing manipulates time and space, creates rhythm and pacing, and may establish visual-aural relationships.

Emulsion. The light-sensitive layer of chemicals fixed to the film base that records the image.

Establishing shot. Captures the scene in a long shot to establish a sense of place.

Eye-level shot. Shows no visible angle, taking an unbiased or neutral position towards the subject.

Eyeline match. The cut is made on the basis of the direction of a character's glance or gaze. In the first shot, a character looks at something offscreen. The next shot shows us what the character sees.

F

Fade in. A technique for beginning a scene whereby the image gradually appears from a blackened screen.

Fade out. A technique for ending a scene whereby the image gradually darkens to black.

Fill light. The light used to balance the shadows of the scene.

Film noir. A French term that refers to the group of gritty, somber thrillers made in the late 1940s and early 1950s. The low-key lighting is particularly distinctive.

Flash forward. A narrative sequence that moves the story from the present to the future.

Flashback. A narrative sequence that moves the action from the present into the past.

Flip frame. The image seems to turn over to reveal another one.

Focal length. The distance in millimeters from the emulsion of the film stock to the center of the camera lens when the lens is focused at infinity. A wide angle lens has a short focal length; a telephoto lens has a long one.

Focus. The degree of sharpness of the image.

Frame. One single image on the film strip. Also refers to the edges of the image projected on the screen.

Framing device. Windows, doorways, and mirrors, as well as other devices that form a frame within the film frame, often draw the spectator's attention to a specific area of the image in order to emphasize what is dramatically, emotionally, or intellectually significant.

Freeze frame. A single frame is reprinted many times so that when projected the shot looks like a still photograph; the action appears to have stopped.

Full shot. A more confined type of long shot. The figure fills the screen from top to bottom of the frame.

G

Genre. A category or type of film that contains similar narrative and visual elements. Preestablished conventions in subject matter, thematic concerns, plot formula, iconography, and style distinguish such genres as the Western, horror film, detective movie, and science fiction film.

Go-motion. A stop-motion technique that allows animated miniatures under electronic control to be in motion while the camera shutter is open, causing a natural blur of motion that adds realism to the shot.

Hairlight. A small spotlight placed behind the subject to illuminate the hair and back of the head, producing a halo effect.

High-angle shot. The camera looks down upon the subject, often suggesting the subject's helplessness and vulnerability.

High-key lighting. This lighting style uses a strong primary light source with a great deal of fill light to create bright, even illumination.

I

Iconography. The likeness or image of an actor or object which imparts a particular meaning to the shot or film.

Intellectual montage. Eisenstein's term for the juxtaposition of two shots that contain differing, contrasting, or seemingly unrelated information to make an abstract idea concrete.

Iris shot. A type of masking shot in which an area in the shape of a circle encloses the image.

J

Jump cut. A slight mismatch between two actions that causes a jarring, disjunctive cut. If the angle of the camera setup does not vary at least 30 degrees from the previous one during the filming of a scene, a jump cut will occur between the two shots. A jump cut also occurs if the projector has ruined a few frames of film, thereby disrupting the shot's continuity.

K

Key light. The primary source of illumination of a set.

Kuleshov effect. Soviet director Lev Kuleshov's experiment in editing. By juxtaposing the same shot of an actor's face with other images, the actor seems to be responding differently to the material in each shot. This proved that editing can "create" a performance.

L

Leitmotif. A musical theme that represents an individual, idea, or personal quality.

Lens. The optical device that controls the size of the subject, the scope of the image, and the range of focus.

Linear perspective. Figures meant to be distant are drawn smaller than those meant to be closer.

Location. An actual place that serves as the background for the action.

Long shot. The camera records an area equal to the height of a standing figure with extensive background, emphasizing the relation between the figure and its surroundings.

Low-angle shot. The camera is placed lower than the subject to produce a towering figure or object. This shot, suggesting the subject's power or authority, may create a heroic or a menacing figure.

Low-key lighting. This lighting style uses a strong primary light source and very little fill light to create areas of high contrast and rich, black shadows.

M

Master shot. The entire scene is filmed in one take without interruption. Close-ups and shots from other angles are added later.

Match cut. The cut is matched on the basis of screen direction, action, graphic elements, or eyeline direction to produce a smooth transition between two shots.

Matte shot. Two separate shots are superimposed and printed onto a single piece of film stock, resulting in a single image. The traveling matte allows for moving images.

Medium shot. The camera records an area equal to the height of a seated figure or a figure from the waist up.

Mise en scène. A French word referring to the organization and arrangement of everything placed in front of the camera in preparation for filming.

Mix. All sounds—dialogue, music, sound effects—on separate tracks are blended electronically or digitally onto a limited number of tracks.

Montage. The French word for editing. Eisensteinian montage refers to assembling shots so that they "collide" with one another and gain new meaning; often quick cutting distinguishes the sequences. In Hollywood the term refers to any sequence of rapidly edited images that suggests the passage of time or events.

Montage of conflict. Sergei Eisenstein's style of editing in which dissimilar images "collide" with one another to produce a meaning greater than the sum of the individual parts.

Morphing. Computer graphics imaging transforms one figure into another.

Motif. A repeated object, action, camera movement, graphic pattern, sound, or phrase.

N

Narrative. A progression of events related in time and by cause; a story.

Normal lens. The lens approximates the scope and size of normal vision.

O

Oblique angle. The camera films from a tilted position to produce a slanted image suggesting tension and trouble. Also called a canted, tilted, or Dutch angle.

Optical printers. Automated machines that are precision-built camera and projector combinations.

P

Pan shot. The camera is mounted on a non-moving base and films while pivoting on its axis, along the line of the horizon from left to right or right to left.

Persistence of vision. The brain retains an image cast on the retina of the eye for a split second after the image has disappeared from view.

Phi phenomenon. A characteristic of human visual perception that allows the spectator to see a series of static images as a single, continuous movement.

Plot. A planned series of interrelated actions that develop and resolve a conflict. The plot establishes the opposing forces and arranges the order of events to build dramatic tension and suspense; a cause-and-effect relationship must exist from one event to the next so that the story advances in a natural and logical manner.

Point of view. Borrowed from literary criticism, the term refers to the "eyes" and "voice" through which a reader or viewer experiences a story or event. First person narrative is generally presented though the device of a voice-over with a dissolve into the past; the spectator must determine if the narrator is reliable or not and how that might affect the outcome of the movie.

Point-of-view shot. Taken from a distance and angle that represents what a character sees. Also called subjective shot or first-person shot.

Process shot. Also called rear projection. The pre-photographed background is projected onto a translucent screen and filmed with live action in the foreground.

Producer. Supervises the overall film project by bringing together the key participants in a package; securing financial backing; selecting the story or screenplay and acquiring the property; choosing the director (who then begins to oversee artistic issues throughout the preproduction phase), the actors, and the crew; and sometimes decides on locations. After making these preliminary decisions, the producer oversees the progress of the project, controls expenditures, and handles all other business details.

Production designer. Also called the art director. Researches decor and settings; oversees artists, craftpersons, and decorators for the creation of a set.

R

Rack focus. Also called pulled focus. Changing focus during a shot without stopping the camera so that an image in one plane gradually blurs as focus is "pulled" to bring detail in another plane into sharp focus.

Rushes. Also called dailies. The selected footage of the day's shooting, which the director and cinematographer usually evaluate before the start of the next day of production.

S

Scene. Refers to a sequence in which the action takes place in a single place and time. The term also means a specific location where a specific set of events occur.

Screen direction. A character, an object, or the camera moves in a specific direction across the screen. Matching shots with the same screen direction establishes continuity.

Screenplay. Serves as the blueprint for the film. The screenwriter plans the structure, plot, characterization, and dialogue.

Self reflexive. A reference to another film, film character, filmmaker, or the process of filmmaking that reminds the viewer that the director has interpreted the material.

Sequence. A shot or series of shots that present a meaningful unit of action.

Set. The "worlds" created in the studio for fiction films.

Setting. The time—historical moment, season, time of day—and the place of the action.

Setup. Placement of the lights and camera in relation to the set, props, and action.

Shooting ratio. The amount of film footage finally used in proportion to the amount discarded.

Shot. The primary unit of filmmaking. A single, uncut length of film.

Shot/reverse shot. A shot sequence often used to record conversations, in which the first shot is followed by another taken from an opposite angle.

Slow motion. The camera films at a faster rate than the normal 24 frames per second (sound film). The image is projected at normal speed so the action looks slow.

Sound effects. All sounds that are not dialogue, narration, or music. They heighten the illusion of reality. Often ambient or background sound not connected to visible sources.

Sound off. Sound whose source is not visible on the screen.

Sound on. Sound whose source is visible on the screen; dialogue or noise made by onscreen figures or objects; for example, a record player or a radio.

Sound stage. Spaces in which acoustics and lighting of sets can be controlled.

Soviet montage. A style of editing distinguished by the combining of seemingly unrelated shots in order to create new, meaningful relationships within the viewer's mind.

Special effect (FX). Any technique or device used to create the illusion of reality in a situation where it is not possible, safe, or economical to achieve the same result with conventional cinematography.

Stop-motion photography. Also called single frame or stop-action photography. The camera exposes one frame at a time, and the position of the object or person is changed between shots. This creates the illusion that an inanimate object can move on its own.

Storyboard. A series of sketches that lays out the setups of the shots.

Structure. The planned framework of a film.

Subjective shot. Also called a point-of-view or first-person shot. This shot presents a character's specific point of view by showing the spectator what the character sees.

Swish pan. A pan so rapid that it blurs the image.

Symbol. A concrete object that stands for an abstract idea.

Synchronous sound. Sound occurring at the same time as the image that produces it.

T

Take. The recording of a shot on film or video. Each time the shot is filmed, it is identified as a "take" by number. When shooting fiction films, shots are often repeated many times.

Telephoto lens. A lens that has a long focal length and minimum depth of field. It flattens the image.

Textual connotation. Meanings that emerge from the organization of a specific work.

Theme. The main idea or ideas of a film that emerge as a function of the interplay among all the narrative, visual, and aural elements.

Three-act dramatic structure. Most narrative films produced in America adhere to an Aristotelian or three-act dramatic structure. Act One introduces the characters and setting. Act Two deals with major plot developments that escalate the conflict between opposing forces. Act Three builds the conflict to a climax, the film's moment of greatest suspense, and then resolves all the loose narrative ends.

Tracking or traveling or trucking shot. Any shot in which the camera moves while filming.

V

Voice-over. Narration or dialogue spoken off camera. Often the disembodied voice gives information, offers explanation or description, or tells a story.

W

Wide-angle shot. A shot taken with a lens of short focal length that produces an image of great scope and increases the illusion of depth. By allowing the foreground, middleground, and background planes to remain in sharp focus at the same time, this shot can create important juxtapositions among people and objects in the various planes.

Wipe. One image moves across the screen, pushing off the one already there.

Z

Zoom shot. A variable-focus lens changes the range of focus and the scope of the shot without stopping the camera during the filming.

Index

Bold page numbers refer to figures.